Ransomware and Cybercrime

In May 2001, Jim Gosler, known as the Godfather and commander of US agencies' cyber offensive capability, said, "Either the Intelligence Community (IC) would grow and adapt, or the Internet would eat us alive." Mr Gosler was speaking at his retirement only several months before the terrorist attacks of 9/11. He possibly did not realise the catalyst or the tsunami that he and his tens of thousands of US IC offensive website operatives had created and commenced.

Over the last two decades, what Mr Gosler and his army of Internet keyboard warriors created would become the *modus operandi* for every faceless, nameless, state-sponsored or individual cybercriminal to replicate against an unwary, ill-protected, and ignorant group of executives and security professionals who knew little to nothing about the clandestine methods of infiltration and weaponisation of the Internet that the US and UK agencies led, all in the name of security.

This book covers many cyber and ransomware attacks and events, including how we have gotten to the point of massive digital utilisation, particularly during the global lockdown and COVID-19 pandemic, to online spending that will see twice the monetary amount lost to cybercrime than what is spent online.

There is little to no attribution, and with the IC themselves suffering cyberattacks, they are all blamed on being sophisticated ones, of course. We are witnessing the undermining of our entire way of life, our economies, and even our liberties. The IC has lots to answer for and unequivocally created the disastrous situation we are currently in. They currently have little to no answer. We need—no, we must demand—change. That change must start by ensuring the Internet and all connections to it are secure and no longer allow easy access and exfiltration for both the ICs and cybercriminals.

Ransomware and Cybercrime

Andrew Jenkinson

CRC Press
Taylor & Francis Group
Boca Raton   London

CRC Press is an imprint of the
Taylor & Francis Group, an **informa** business

First Edition published 2022
by CRC Press
6000 Broken Sound Parkway NW, Suite 300, Boca Raton, FL 33487–2742

and by CRC Press
4 Park Square, Milton Park, Abingdon, Oxon, OX14 4RN

CRC Press is an imprint of Taylor & Francis Group, LLC

© 2022 Taylor & Francis Group, LLC

ISBN: 978-1-032-23549-3 (hbk)
ISBN: 978-1-032-23550-9 (pbk)
ISBN: 978-1-003-27821-4 (ebk)

DOI: 10.1201/9781003278214

Contents

Foreword

My name is Dr Vladas Leonas, I am an Adjunct Professor at Torrens University and I have over 45 years of experience in technology and over 20 years of experience in cybersecurity. I have often been concerned and even frustrated by the lack of understanding and knowledge, and therefore the lack of action to secure corporate businesses and even government entities, and, in my own way, have been vocal to get my views across.

I met the author, Andy Jenkinson about 2 years ago and immediately identified with his position, with what he stood for and the way he tried to simplify the messages and oversights. Andy is unquestionably a thought leader that not only Talks the Talk with unbridled volume, but like no one else as I have witnessed, Walks the Walk.

I took great pleasure in reviewing Andy's first book, "Stuxnet to Sunburst" and even with all my years of experience there was a plethora of information that I was unaware of and that resonated with me. When Andy asked me to write a foreword for his second book Ransomware & Cybercrime, I was delighted to do so.

The title, like the real thing, is going on all around us, from fast food chains, to nuclear warhead providers, the consequences are immense and yet every next day they look like yesterday's news, it is all seemingly taken with a pinch of salt. As Andy says, what will it take to make the world and its leaders to wake up from their slumber, I am unsure, however 2021 will see Cyber and Ransomware attacks amounting to a total estimated cost, and loss, of $6 trillion making it equivalent to the world's third largest economy! Leaders need to awaken before it is simply too late!

It is 2021 and it is hard to find a person who hasn't heard about Ransomware, as the number of Ransomware attacks is growing exponentially. But how much do you know about these attacks?

The book that you have just opened contains not only a comprehensive collection of Ransomware attacks and their history. It goes much deeper.

It is a collection of study cases that illustrates evolution of Ransomware attacks and also offers deep insights in arrogance and negligence (should I say criminal negligence?) of numerous Boards, CEOs and CISOs that have been warned about their vulnerable Internet positions and still done nothing to fix it. Nothing! Even when they have been shown vulnerabilities remaining after the breaches that they have already suffered from!

These vulnerabilities have been explored and weaponized over the years through offensive efforts by various agencies and by now they have become the very first attack surfaces for cyber criminals and nation actors. What are these vulnerabilities? Firstly – unprotected (not managed, abandoned, but still active) domains and subdomains, expired certificates and use of HTTP (but not HTTPS). They are so easy to fix, but they still stay wide open for exploitation by evil-minded groups.

Material in the book (and it includes some very interesting examples of mail trails) clearly illustrates that certain entities in charge of national security are not willing to let go of their offensive capabilities and thus are shying away from providing adequate advice to the industry in general and especially to CNI players.

Unfortunately, a lot of CEOs and CISOs still think mainly in terms of end-point protection, while other open doors still stay outside their vision field, though these open doors are extremely dangerous! Especially, when we are talking about CNI. Convergence between IT and OT has already shown that attack on IT via the above-mentioned attack surfaces can laterally move onto OT bringing far reaching consequences. And unless Boards, CEOs and CISOs start to take

Internet-facing security seriously and address glaring holes there, no one will be spared in this war – be it McDonalds, a large insurance company, a supplier to the US nuclear ammunition, or an SME, especially in the current environment of rapidly growing popularity of Ransomware-as a-Service offerings (like REvil) accompanied by "segregation of duties" between several groups of cyber criminals.

Recent galore of so-called digital transformations (and massive proliferation of the agile approach) together with consequences of COVID-19 (e. g. work from home) significantly increased companies' exposure to the Internet and, subsequently, the risk of cyber-attacks.

I feel obliged to add couple of words about the author. Andy Jenkinson is a highly respected professional and is well known around the industry. He is a Group CEO of CIP specialising in Risk, Compliance, Cyber Security and PKI. Through our online collaboration over the last couple of years I have personally witnessed his tireless efforts to educate people and to help various organisations out. I have also witnessed multiple push backs that never stopped Andy's efforts. Andy is a sought-after speaker and has spoken at numerous conferences and events. Andy is also the author of another outstanding book "Stuxnet to Sunburst. 20 Years of Digital Exploitation and Cyber Warfare" that I can also strongly recommend.

Who should read this book? In my opinion, it is a must read for Chairmen, Board Members, CEOs and CISOs, as well as, to those in charge of operational security. Anyone interested in cyber security will also enjoy (and may be frightened) reading this book. In summary – I can strongly recommend this book to wide audience of anyone with interest in this area!

Dr Vladas Leonas
Adjunct Professor, Torrens University

Preface

It is not the strongest that survive—it is those who are the most adaptable.

In the world of Ransomware and cybercrime, we are witnessing an unprecedented shift in terms of both power and flexibility by our adversaries. The digital world and consequently the entire world's weaknesses and vulnerabilities are being laid bare by the very same digital tools designed to confirm security. OSINT (Open-Source Intelligence) technology, often free, is being used to identify exposed and exploitable domains and subdomains that lack controls, management, and security. Throughout history, what was designed and developed for offensive capability and used in warfare could also be used for defensive capability.

It is fair to say the odds are most certainly stacked against us currently; however, we, as a profession and as a race, are doing very little to change this position and continuing to ignore the facts right in front of us. The result of this is Ransomware and cyberattacks on a level that is a challenge to keep track of, let alone fight against with any real gusto. Furthermore, because of that continued lack of domain security, even post-breach and even after the root cause has been identified, all attempts to improve the already sub optimal and insecure position are futile. As soon as new devices, laptops, servers, and so on are connected, they can be immediately compromised.

With near mass hysteria and daily breaches being confirmed, many companies, sporting events and situations that resulted in mass gatherings were stopped because of the COVID-19 pandemic. However, that also created and added to an already woefully insecure position and presented many major opportunities and challenges, not least of which was Remote Access that exacerbated today's already insecure positions.

With the opportunity of staff working from home and remote locations, connecting via unsecured connections and receiving many spoof, malicious emails confirming what to do re COVID-19 and so on, many of those messages were unknowingly carrying Malware code (Trojans) and gaining deep-rooted access to more enterprises. The German government was caught out to the tune of 100 million Euro in a two-week period by a spoof, copycat website that collated then claimed COVID-19 financial support and the German Government, unknowingly obliged paying the monies to cyber criminals instead of real claimants and people that required financial support.

The losses just keep increasing. Last year Travelex owner Finablr, which had its Initial Public Offering (IPO) in May 2019 for around $3 billion, suffered a breach in December 2019, just months later, were placed in Administration under Price Waterhouse Coopers (PWC) in April 2020 and then sold for $1 in December 2020. This shocking tale should serve as a major alarm bell (Klaxons) of just what can happen, and how quickly. I suspect no Risk Management could never predict such a situation, and also I suspect a lot of Investors had plenty to write off... British Airways (BA) also announced major changes to avoid collapse following their data breach of nearly 0.5 million and an original ICO (Information Commissioner's Office) fine of £128 million.

We know company's worth $billions will have associated costs with revenues of around 70%. Many other companies will be trading with massive deficits for some period following COVID-19; many will simply cease trading.

In discussions and following research within the cyber insurance sector, it became very apparent that Insurers are seemingly quite happy with their lot; however, in the last two months both CNA and AXA have suffered breaches, highlighting their own insecure positions. CNA went on to pay $40 million in ransom. These Insecure positions both organisations seem to be content to ignore and continue to maintain. However, can they really fail to understand the math of business? The cyber-insurance market is predicted to increase to over $200 billion; however, when laid over the total of predicted losses of $6 trillion in 2021 and predicted to surpass $10 trillion by 2025, there is a clear, massive gulf between the two figures.

For example, Company A has revenues of $1 billion. From that $1 billion, 35% will be used to pay staff ($350 million). A further 25% will pay overhead, buildings, and general day-to-day costs ($250 million). A further 10% will be needed to be used to pay for technology, security, and potential losses. Leaving capital adequacy aside for one minute, that leaves a total of 30% or, in the case of Company A, $300 million before any taxes.

Now consider Company A is a cyber insurance underwriter and they have total revenues of $1 billion. If total claims ever exceed the aforementioned 30%, that is, $300 million, they are trading at a loss. Let us not forget they are in business to make a profit and must be able to prove capital adequacy for such situations that might arise. It is quite a fine balance for sure and may be a major reason for AXA in France confirming they will no longer 'guarantee' customers that they will meet Ransomware settlements a week before being breached themselves by Ransomware…

Any way you look at it and regardless of how many companies will 'share' the annual accumulated losses, many companies will simply be unable to survive these losses and can do one of two things. Leaders can either prepare for their company's demise or proactively better prepare to prevent being attacked and the substantial losses. When it comes to Critical National Infrastructure, Healthcare, and Financial Services, there should not be an option; however, there is still so much ignorance of real security, and even the plausible deniability card is still played.

There are two types of companies, just as there are two types of leaders: those that want to make a difference in the medium to long term and those that want to make an annual bonus and take their leave at the appropriate time. You can see which is which on both counts and in many companies.

It is fair to say that unless you know or can see what you are trying to protect, you might just as well be at war wearing a blindfold and without the right tools to protect yourself or indeed the business.

Make no mistake, we are all at cyberwar and none of us have the option to become a conscientious objector or opt out. If you or your organisation uses technology in any form whatsoever, you are on the front line, like it or not. Outsourcing is always an option; however, you cannot outsource accountability or responsibility. The legal boys will simply start with their Class Action Lawsuits and tie up organisations and people with more time and associated costs.

We are fast approaching the middle of 2021, and the GDP for the entire world has been dramatically reduced, that is, apart from one country, China. It is widely known and accepted that China wants to become the Number 1 Economic power from their current Number 2 position. It is also widely known and accepted that 80% of all cyberattacks are against US companies, governments, CNIs, and so on as the United States is more reliant upon digital devices and the Internet. It is no coincidence that website proliferation is directly tracked and matched by the proliferation of cyberattacks and $losses over the last decade. When laid over each other, the upward curve is near identical.

So, the choice is ours. We can either continue floundering in the wake of attack after attack and being busy fools or make sure we are secure facing and connected to the Internet to prevent easy infiltration. Websites and the Internet were designed to aid our daily lives, communications, and business. Sadly, due to the massive focus, originally by the CIA, National Security Agency (NSA), and Government Communications Headquarters (GCHQ), of mass digital data collection and also, over the last decade or so, by adversaries, the Internet and website connectivity have been weaponised and threatened our very way of life. Due to the actions of our governments and agencies 20 years ago, they are in no hurry, bizarrely, to bolster this critical security area and are stuck at a crossroads. They should come clean and disclose the facts about one of the world's worst kept secrets and encourage everyone to take Internet security as opposed to encouraging people to ignore it, in order to facilitate their own clandestine activities, which are proven to be the root cause of the majority of cyberattacks, or continue burying their heads in the sand. One must ask if the good guys just simply became the bad guys; just who are the owners of all the breached but government-contracted cyber security organisations, and who really owns all the bitcoin wallets? The United

States and Israel to this day, over a decade on, still do not own up to the world's first digital act of war...

Our economy, let alone the human suffering, is being challenged like never before, and we have a very limited time to address it. Has it tipped the balance of scales already? Currently cybercrime costs and losses account for around 10% of the world's GDP and will continue rising. That is a sobering thought and write off for everyone and poses major issues for the entire world.

This book, the second in a series, follows on from Stuxnet to Sunburst, 20 years of digital exploitation and cyberwar, and covers more complex examples of what is really happening, how it is facilitated, and what must happen before it is too late. Ransomware has multiplied many times over in the last several years, and it is all too easy to see why. Within a week of the latest Ransomware breach at Colonial Pipeline, insider knowledge suggests this company, critical to the East Coast of the United States, may well have paid the $30 million ransom demand. The total cost will potentially be ten times this amount, and yet they remain open to being breached again due to maintaining their insecure (possibly unknown) positions...

1

STUXNET TO SUNBURST AND RANSOMWARE DEVELOPMENT

My previous book, *Stuxnet to Sunburst, 20 Years of Digital Exploitation and Cyberwarfare*, took the reader on a journey and looked at numerous specific cyberattacks and the first use of digital code for warfare in the form of Stuxnet. Stuxnet used digital certificates laced with malicious code (Stuxnet). It went in depth about many attacks and concluded with the similarities of the SolarWinds breach that started in early 2020 and surfaced in December 2020, affecting thousands of clients including the US government. What made this ironic is SolarWinds is an American company that develops software to help manage clients' networks, infosec, and infrastructure. As a well-known and highly utilised US government supplier, SolarWinds could not have been better placed to be breached and cause maximum infiltration, disruption, and unfettered access. What made it a double whammy, in many ways, was the fact that once Domain Administration Access had been achieved via a hijacking a legacy, insecure subdomain, the adversaries laced SolarWinds' own digital certificates, which were distributed and used to update customers' versions, with Sunburst, the name given to the code. Furthermore, the delay of 13 days from update acceptance, often without any intervention, was an identical timeframe as used in Stuxnet was set before Sunburst was activated. Is that just a coincidence with Stuxnet's own 13-day delay from infiltration? We think not.

Both Stuxnet and Sunburst were cyberattacks with a specific purpose. The first was to destabilise, slow down, or even halt the Iranian nuclear program, the second to cause major disruption and infiltrate the US government, including the Treasury. This can only be a bad thing as the United States, indeed all organisations and governments, do not have proper controls or know what their enterprise contains; chances are they contain much more now, along with data exfiltration.

DOI: 10.1201/9781003278214-1

Over the last few years, organised crime has watched, and learned, from how simply, and anonymously similar attacks can be utilised as part of their overall illegal business plans. In fact, they are so easy that digital cyberattacks have overtaken and surpassed all other forms of crime and are so successful as organised crime, they are in fact much better organised than the people charged with ensuring security. It is also not unreasonable to confirm that the good guys have to secure 100% and the bad guys find a single access point. This situation was further exacerbated by revelations in 2013 by Edward Snowden and others who confirmed the access points and tools used to infiltrate organisations and governments to gain digital access and exfiltrate information and data. The harvesting of this data gave control and power; however, once it fell into the wrong hands, the birth and early iterations of Ransomware were spawned, and the global market and economy would change forever...

What is Ransomware? In the simplest of terms, Ransomware is the name given to a type of Malware from crypto virology that typically threatens to publish the victims' data or block access to it unless a ransom is paid. As we know, a person being held hostage and not released until a ransom is paid is highly illegal. In the digital world, it is seemingly tolerated, even accepted, which is why organisations like Darkside, who hit Colonial recently, have received an estimated $90 million over the last several months...

Ransomware has evolved over the last few years, even more so over the last year or so, and now it typically means cybercriminals exfiltrate data to then demonstrate to the victim the data is in their possession and to prove they have been able to remove it. They offer to sell it back at a premium, and so the next attack commences. Let us look at this closer, as it is an area that even some of the biggest and best leaders in security don't fully understand. In or around 2013/2014, Google and others wanted to move from the weak HTTP (Hypertext Transfer Protocol) to HTTPS to ensure better and stronger security for website visitors. The S part of HTTPS effectively stood for security and meant all data would be encrypted as opposed to being kept in plaintext form. Plaintext form is text as you are reading here, hopefully easily understood for everyone. You will be familiar with various emails and communication Apps such as Whatsapp, Signal, and so on. These have all been designed with the same purpose in mind, to ensure messages are encrypted and enable only decryption by the recipient, or that was at least their desired business plan at the outset.

What Google possibly never realised is that not everyone would adopt this great new security position, and what took years to agree on, design, and develop for global increased security would in fact make it even easier to identify organisations that were not using the new variant of HTTPS and, as such, were maintaining data in plaintext form. It would become a cybercriminal's staple diet to go to organisations who maintained HTTP and enable easy access, plaintext data enabling them to encrypt it and demand a ransom for the decryption capability properly. Google confirmed they would share details of those that ignored the upgraded HTTPS by showing a Not Secure text in the address bar. The list of organisations that have fallen foul of such oversight or negligence reads like a who's who of governments, Fortune 500, and FTSE 100 companies.

It gets worse. The HTTPS element refers to the digital certificate validity; that is, does have the correct certificate and is valid. It matches the domain and is it of the correct type. What it does not tell you is whether the domain is configured correctly or has other security vulnerabilities that are exploitable. Does it use a hosting provider, shared services, DNS (Domain Name System) or CDN (Content Delivery Network) third party content, and so on?

The self-inflicted challenge is rarely understood, and that shamelessly includes Captains of Industry and far too many Chief Security Information Officers. This is enough cause for concern, as although maintaining a Not Secure domain confirms a total lack of Internet security controls and management, it also highlights a lack of internal security by default. Furthermore, it also confirms that domains are being published, often using third-party content, hosting providers with shared responsibilities, or servers using older code written in HTTP which relegates the entire site to being Not Secure. Unauthenticated, lacking data integrity, and data often in plaintext: it is easy to see why 200,000 websites of the 1.2 billion each day are targeted and attacked and why successful attacks are costing the global economy $billions, ever $trillions annually.

In the last 12–24 months, my associates all around the world have been sending me details of local Ransomware attacks. From Healthcare in Australia, New Zealand, the United States, Ireland, the United

Kingdom, and many more. It used to trickle through at the rate of around 4 or 5 per week; now it is that many daily. It would take a full-time analyst just to record all the Ransomware attacks alone, let alone the monies paid.

In 2019, a meeting of the US Senate Committee first agreed that paying Ransomware was unacceptable and would lead to further crimes, and they were not wrong. Further Bills have tried to be passed making Ransomware payments banned. It stops short of making it illegal, and even Insurance companies, until very recently, were willing to pay Ransomware as part of the overall policy and often would take an active role in negotiations. Now, call me crazy, but is this simply a blatant reshuffling of monies from A to B and allowing further crimes to manifest? Furthermore, every company we have researched that has been breached has sub optimal, insecure domains, making them exposed, vulnerable, and easily exploited. This fact alone should nullify their insurance coverage and policy, and yet in one example, University Hospital of New Jersey paid $675,000 whilst maintaining a Not Secure homepage, agreed to the payment of Ransomware with their Insurance providers and state, and remain Not Secure some nine months later. ... Their Not Secure position acted as a beacon for Cybercriminals, and they paid and continued to ignore the root cause.

Being very candid, most companies simply ignore basic security and then get breached. It is like smoking and ignoring the warnings on the side of the packet or driving blindfolded and expecting nothing to happen.

RTFs (Ransomware Task Forces) have recently been set up, which one would hope is a step forward, as is the EO (Executive Order) by the Biden Administration of ploughing a further $500 million into cyber security with the NSA being heavily focused upon. Our reservation, indeed, our concern, is that our two messages to the RTF have been ignored, even after sharing intelligence of their own, and their panel's websites running Fs and 0s for Internet security. Their, and seemingly others', focus is very much about Ransomware management and simply not enough about prevention; however, given their own security posture, I guess that speaks volumes. As for the NSA, it has long been known that since the terrorist attacks of 9/11, their focus has shifted immensely from data harvesting at a ratio of more than 1–100 of defensive resources to offensive. As such, Ransomware continues and indeed increases. As Paul Nakasone said to the Senate Committee, 'Our adversaries do not fear us'. Given our frequent research and findings, candy from a baby spring to mind.

In addition, when organisations supported by the DOD, DHS, RTF, MITRE CWE, and thousands of others happily maintain sub optimal security, they have not only made themselves a target but an easily exploitable one. We often advise clients when such situations occur, even though it may be uncomfortable: was the attack down to someone being complacent or complicit? Bitcoin and other digital currencies coupled with Blockchains enable a degree of anonymity and one simply cannot be sure who the good, and who the bad guys really are. Security is truly a choice, as is smoking, drinking, or being reckless. Domain security is critical and overlooked systemically and ignored across sector after sector. Ransomware and cyberattacks are a self-fulfilling prophecy. Ransomware is rarely sophisticated, as it is always termed to mask incompetence and complacency. It is time to call it as it is before it is simply too late.

There are two distinct ways to decrease the chances of being the victim of a cyberattack and Ransomware. The first is simply unthinkable in today's digital world, and that is to disconnect everything from the Internet and go back to pen, paper, and speaking directly with each other. Or making sure the organisation controls and manages Internet-facing and connected security. Ask yourself: why do most agencies take this area seriously and, in the main, have security at this critical area covered? They know all too well that this is the first access point from an adversary thousands of miles away; that thin cable with a connection will punish anyone who neglects their domain/server security. We explored several governments cyberattacks in the previous book due to insecurity, and we will look at several Ransomware attacks in this book, and by the end of it, you will be shocked, in disbelief, and possibly a tad paranoid about just what our governments initiated and are doing to prevent this downward spiral and trajectory they started 20 years ago...

2
Not Secure, F and 0...

We have over a hundred domains, we run bug scanning daily and fully appreciate the critical security issues and requirements of domains and security. We know some are literally holding pages with little to no data, we also know the top two dozen or so that we control and manage.

(CISO of a US $billion cyber security firm 20 May 2021.
after numerous cyberattacks, including SolarWinds)

So, I asked my vulnerabilities and research team to have a look. Within an hour, they sent me a dozen insecure domains belonging to the company. Even worse, Not Secure Login domains, domains with mismatching Transport Layer Security (TLS) certificates, TLS that had expired, and misconfigured domains.

As a matter of professional courtesy, I sent two screen shots to the CISO at 23:00 hrs my time in the United Kingdom to show them the findings. To the first, they responded, 'Thanks for that, luckily that is only a client demo site', implying it had no data or security exposure. On the second, a company videoconferencing Not Secure domain used by hundreds of the company's staff constantly and totally open to a Man-in-the-Middle Attack, no comment was made...

We hear dozens of excuses or reasons maintaining Not Secure domains is an OK thing; it is simply not. Any domain with a company on it that has been allowed to fall into a situation of relying upon obsolete TLS certificates at the absolute best demonstrates to anyone looking that the company lacks Internet security controls and management. What is also overlooked is the fact that cyber criminals are scanning the Internet looking for F and 0 rated websites to add to their target list and launch attacks on. Put simply, a Not Secure website says a lot about a company's overall security position and capability. If it is insecurely connected to the Internet, chances are it is not much better on the inside. Equally, as the SolarWinds breach clearly showed

DOI: 10.1201/9781003278214-2

the world, in a single domain hijacking and takeover, some lateral movement and you can lace digital certificates with Sunburst malicious code and breach thousands of companies.... It is not clear which part of digital open doors people fail to understand or secure; however, our research has discovered the same situation at leading global Insurance providers, including cyber insurance providers, financial service regulators, central banks, and even our own GCHQ and NCSC, and No. 10 Downing Street.

Let us consider physical premises for a moment. Let us say the same company, the previous cyber security company, had premises instead of domains. Would they have the same attitude of only making sure a couple dozen of their premises were secure, locked up, and alarmed, or would they say they only lock up a couple dozen? Of course, they would lock them all up, and yet when it comes to their digital, online, 24 × 7 domains, seemingly it does not matter. This poor view and complacency is exactly why cyberattacks are occurring constantly and are unchallenged.

In the address bar of every website, you will see www.example.com. In front of it, you will see either a padlock, confirming a valid TLS certificate and the fact it is using the latest HTTPS protocol. If it is not, it will display a Not Secure text instead. To complicate matters even more, even when a padlock is displayed, it does not mean the domain is secure and safe; it simply confirms the validity of the certificate. This confusion extends to numerous security professionals. Let me explain further. We recently informed many organisations of their overall insecure positions recently, including Lloyd's of London, the global Insurance leaders. Their CEO and CISO rebutted that they had scanned using SSL Labs, who had found the certificate valid and rated them at A+. They did not understand or comprehend why a full domain and server hosting that domain was different and subsequently dismissed the F and 0 Rating, even when presented with evidence of major concerns, anomalies, and issues related to their security and making them insecure, including cookies, code injection, sub-resource impact (often code that covers the overall site), cross-site scripting, and so on. These two intelligent people, and many more, were relying on less than 5% of the components that make up a domain to satisfy themselves they were secure when, clearly, they were not and remain not... We always say that no security professional should ever take an SSL test in isolation as a misconfigured domain will nullify the SSL test. This creates, as the Lloyds team, a False Positive that is worthless.

The challenge continues inasmuch that far too many people do not understand the complexities of websites, including the website owners themselves and all too frequently web developers. A website typically uses numerous third-party components: graphics, tables, text, and so on. This content is not always checked for security, and web developers pull in various images, data, and the like often without checking. The website looks and does exactly what everyone wanted; however, it may not have been checked for security, and then it is made live, often insecurely. Additionally, the company hosting the website, usually on a shared server, may also make the already compromised website live as soon as it is hosted. It is not uncommon—in fact let me rephrase that—it is quite common to find servers with numerous security issues and legacy CVEs (Common Vulnerabilities and Exposures), some dating back for years and unknown to the hosting company because they too are not looking at security but selling price-sensitive hosting services. Then add DNS (Domain Name System) and CDN (Content Delivery Network), the majority of which have been targeted and successfully attacked as Agency favourite exploits and Backdoors and you can see why websites can be and are weaponised and used for nefarious reasons.

During COVID-19 in 2020, the German government launched a website to support and provide funding for German businesses to claim monies to support them during lockdowns. The site was launched and had several issues. Subsequently, a second 'Evil Twin' Shadow website was set up by cybercriminals, it was identical. Identical apart from one thing: instead of being owned and managed by the German government, it was an illegal Shadow site. For several weeks, the second website ran, and some business owners logged in to one site, others unknowingly to the Shadow site. Business owners completed the various forms and data required to make the COVID-19 claims for financial support in the same way for weeks. The Pandemic and urgency of supporting thousands and thousands of businesses was key, and staff at the government were overwhelmed and also being hampered. After a period of two months, millions upon millions of Euros had been distributed to businesses; however, sometime later when swathes of people voiced their anger and concerns about completing all the documentation online only to receive no support, did the truth emerge. Around half of the business owners had completed their details and claims on the Shadow site. That data was taken by the cyber criminals and re-sent to the real website with just one change, the bank account details. It was estimated at the time that some 100 million Euros had, over a several-week period, been incorrectly paid to cybercriminals making falsified claims using real people's data.

This story is far from unique. We wrote about the Vatican's Not Secure homepages following their breach last summer and the fact that due to COVID-19, the followers, that is, all 1.3 billion Catholic followers of the Church and the Vatican, were forced online during the Pandemic. That includes being kept updated, supporting their faith, and of course making donations. The Vatican had fallen into the trap thousands, possibly millions, of organisations do, and that is to overlook or ignore the critical security of their domains. We researched the Vatican, and not only did the Homepage rely upon an obsolete SSL certificate, but so did 82 other websites out of a total of 85 websites. This meant many were totally exposed, highly vulnerable, and easily exploitable. It also meant that due to the PII (Personally Identifiable Information), it was in breach of General Data Protection Regulation (GDPR) regulations. By being in breach of GDPR, the Vatican could be fined up to 4% of their annual income. As, indeed, so could the German government in the previous scenario.

A similar situation happened when British Airways were breached a few years ago when an illegal redirect website captured the data and sold nearly half a million bogus flights when BAWays.com was nefariously set up for six days, totally unbeknown to BA. BA were originally fined £128 million for the breach, which was subsequently greatly reduced to £20 million by the ICO due to market conditions and COVID-19. BA later borrowed £500 million from the British government.

Then there was Travelex, owned by FINABLR. Travelex floated on the London Stock Exchange in May 2019 for around $3 billion to great fanfare. On 31 December, Travelex were victims of a Ransomware attack. By mid-January, Travelex paid a reported £5 million to the Ransomware gang, and two weeks after that addressed the obsolete TLS cert their homepage was relying upon and that we had informed them of on 2 January. We can only speculate if they floated whilst maintaining a Not Secure position on their homepage; however, as usual, in such a situation, they were alerting cyber criminals who constantly look for the Fs and 0s to attack, and Travelex fitted that *Modus Operandi* perfectly. Several months later, the breach was compounded by a near-global lockdown due to Covid-19, and Travelex, 11 months after floating for $3 billion, went into Administration under Price Waterhouse Coopers. Travelex continued treading water for several more months and was eventually sold in December 2020 for the princely sum of $1... A tale of Boom to Cyber Bust in 18 months.

No longer can a cyberattack or Ransomware breach be considered a nuisance or inconvenient. It can, and will bring £billion businesses down, as Travelex had proven. We constantly hear of Executives and Boards saying they do not understand the issues of cyber or what needs to be done. I candidly suggest they start learning, and quickly. In addition, the so-called experts, as in the case of Lloyd's of London, that are relying upon 'expertise' really need to acknowledge they simply do not know everything and that by ignoring the fundamental basics, they are placing themselves, the business, the shareholders, and partners at totally unnecessary risk. Risks that can lead to the collapse of their company...

CASE STUDY 1

HTTP to HTTPS addition

Today we hear much about Digital Trust and even Zero Trust (ZT). Both have become fashionable terms. In truth, they are critical; however, few companies appreciate their real meaning, and digital and zero trust are often little more than terms and yardsticks to obtain larger budgets, which far too many continue spending unwisely and squander and which make little, to no real security difference. Today all companies MUST consider the trust they provide their customers; however, major organisations and governments are falling short of basic, fundamental security. There is a long way to go until such positions such as

Digital and Zero Trust are a reality. One only has to see the number of cyber and Ransomware attacks and fines for privacy negligence. Put simply, digital trust and regulators are at best an irritation, and the losers are, as always, the public. WARNING: sooner or later people will vote with their feet…

In 2014, Google and other Internet Service Providers (ISPs) said enough is enough and decided to try and make the Internet safer and more secure. That statement and decision alone confirm that it was not and, sadly, still is not. The strategy was formulated and sought to move from the traditional HTTP to HTTPS, the S standing for Secure. The decision saw the move from unencrypted data in transit to encrypted traffic. The plan was unquestionably a step in the right direction but had several failings. The first failing was the migration to HTTPS required full adoption; it took until 2018 to actually gain worthwhile support and adoption. Finally, in 2018, companies and organisations that did not adopt HTTPS would be publicly shamed by their websites displaying the *Not Secure* text in the address bar instead of a padlock. This would become known as a shaming of companies that were not taking their security or the security of their customers or potential customers seriously. Sadly, although the situation has improved, the 1000-plus companies that we have researched and that suffered cyber or Ransomware attacks all maintained sub optimal and insecure websites, many still do. … There is no coincidence.

The challenge with this is if we look at cyber and Ransomware attacks and consider what that attack is looking for, we can see how unencrypted (plaintext) data is an unrivalled appeal to cybercriminals bolstered by more stringent and stricter Privacy Laws, and losses have often covered by ignorant cyber insurance providers. Plaintext data, once exfiltrated, often because it is being sent using HTTP, is easily captured and then used to hold a victim to ransom due to having Personally Identifiable Information. In 2018, when address bars displayed Not Secure, it also signalled and confirmed unencrypted data traffic. What was intended to make the world more secure was in fact used to identify those that were weak and exploitable. In addition, here in 2021, a full three years later, those organisations are also confirming they are not controlling or managing their website, server, and web interfaces when displaying a Not Secure text, and cybercriminals swarm like sharks around a kill. Not adopting HTTPS is a very poor, unwise, and lax position for any company to maintain, and for three years, the entire world has been informed of such poor practice when seeing the Not Secure text. It is a situation that, if those in charge of the business knew of it, they would certainly not ignore. It impacts every user and customer both up and downstream. Yet far too many so-called security experts overlook, ignore, and neglect such positions but are all too willing to state they spent $millions on security and declare they are secure to the Board and Executives who know no better.

To understand the move from HTTP to HTTPS, let's list the key terms:

- **HTTP (Hypertext Transfer Protocol)**—The foundation of online communication (how information is sent from a server to a browser).
- **HTTPS (Hypertext Transfer Protocol Secure)**—HTTP improved and with an encrypted layer of security (S).
- **Encryption**—Encoding information so it's only accessible by authorised parties and not plaintext, the latter being the staple diet of cybercriminals.
- **SSL (Secure Sockets Layer)**—Technology protocol that creates encrypted communication links between servers and browsers.
- **SSL Certificate**—Data files that encrypt digital information and activate secure connections when installed on web servers.
- **DNS (Domain Name System)**—Directory of domain names that are translated to IP addresses.

Google and other ISPs cited three distinct reasons to move from HTTP to HTTPS. They wanted to have the websites and owners matched and authenticated; to ensure the data had integrity and was not altered or tampered with; and finally, all data in flight would be encrypted, ensuring it was not in plaintext. These three reasons alone were in themselves excellent reasons, and Google unequivocally drove the market. It is particularly important until that point, offensive website expertise could simply infiltrate pretty much any website and did so with a plethora of attack vectors such as Man in the Middle (MiTM), Drive by attack, Waterhole attacks, code injection, and so on. Now at least those that are indeed secure have vastly improved their odds not to be targeted. As the old saying goes, I do not need to outrun the hungry lion, just outrun you...

The vast majority of companies that now suffer attacks are those that have either not migrated to HTTPS, have misconfigured subdomains, or that have left subdomains using partial HTTP or content from third parties who themselves, due to their own insecure positions, can relegate their clients' websites due to their websites being the weakest link and the path of least resistance, like a domino effect. In addition, using deprecated SSL or TLS V 1.0 and V 1.1 that were both deprecated in 2018 due to known security weaknesses and being east-easy to exploit. A website, or group of websites, are similar to a chain, and only as strong as the weakest link, and the majority of a company's websites collect, collate, and share data; a cybercriminal does not need to crack the secure website, just the insecure connected one...

One final word on HTTP to HTTPS: it is critically important to understand that just the adoption of the appropriate SSL or TLS alone does not guarantee a website's security in isolation. This area, although critical, may be a result of numerous other issues such as misconfiguration, mismatched certificates, or third-party content. It is a situation that requires constant control and management, as the Dev Ops team building, altering, or changing a website's content, or that new product launch or merger bringing websites together, may not necessarily understand, or bother to check the security of the newly published websites. We witness brand-new websites, tier 1 banks, central banks, and governments, regularly making these errors every day. Many might debate the significance, then scurry around trying to cover their tracks and remediate their insecure over-sights. Websites are like a living breathing digital animal. They need constant attention; they are NOT a fit and forget, and those organisations that adopt such a strategy are the very same organ-isations that suffer one of those 'Sophisticated attacks', just like the thousands of others, via their insecure and frequently Not Secure websites using HTTP or other security faux pas… A final word, security of a homepage does not flow up, or downstream to connected subdomains, however, insecurity of a subdomain that is connected, will enable access upstream to a secure homepage. You do not have to enter through a front door to gain access, you can just as easily go via the insecure backdoor to get to the front.

3

RANSOMWARE LESSONS BEING LEARNED...

A year ago this month, in May 2020, we decided to undertake and commenced a full-United States, fifty-state-wide research program to ascertain exactly what the Internet security position of each state was pre the 2020 US election. We had already researched dozens and dozens of breached companies and unequivocally proven the correlation between sub optimal domain security that was public facing and connected to the Internet and breaches. The research and findings were most certainly alarming and confirmed our suspicions. When security is systemically neglected by companies, including governments, which included their critical voting systems, breaches are the result. Donald Trump himself was breached, and our research showed that several of his personal domains as the US President were insecure and broke various privacy laws, as the majority did not provide security for those visiting the domains as well as contributing to his Presidency campaign. As with all our research, we capture screenshots which are dated and evidence, just in case of any disputes, or for Class Actions where we act as Expert Witnesses.

In the summer of 2020, we completed this research and even assisted the FBI as we literally stumbled, as part of the overall program, across a Korean DNS within the US Central Vote. gov system. In essence, the information of many of the millions of US adult voting population could have been harvested and sent out East. No one, including the FBI, had any knowledge of this infiltration. This systemic lack of visibility, security, controls, and management shows a very concerning and worrying position for the US government, who, like it or not, account for around 80% of all known cyberattacks.

DOI: 10.1201/9781003278214-3

So, What Has This to Do with Ransomware?

Let us consider why companies are targeted with Ransomware attacks in the first place. The first thing to understand is that many attacks by adversaries are against companies unknown to them, never visited or communicated with, yet because of the fact they have insecure Internet connectivity, they are flagged. The process of elimination of whom and whom not to attack may vary; however, size of organisation, accounts and reach into partners, and/or governments may play a part in selecting those who are more than likely to pay quickly and who can afford it. What is not lost is how the attacks are being focussed more and more on larger companies who simply cannot afford to have their technology systems down or production ceased such as Colonial Pipeline (more on them later) and Sony. Ransomware demands have dramatically increased to now be tens of $millions and paid. The criminals know that every day out of production for, say, a Colonial will have massive cost implications, and two-thirds of gas companies running out of fuel also adversely stimulates the masses to demand action…

Ransomware is simply a case of criminal activity in the digital realm and world that preys on the insecure to gain access (infiltrate), and then exfiltrate plaintext data (unencrypted due to not being secure). Then share said captured data with their victims, then encrypt it and sell it back, with a ransom payment demanded for the decryption key. CNIs, Health Care operators, and transport organisations, even governments—immaterial of one's personal views, it is all too easy to pay Ransomware to cover one's errors and negligence. What is then frequently and totally overlooked is the root cause. The insecure domains and positions that made the organisation a target and easily exploited in the first place are further ignored and overlooked. ransom is paid, and the insecurity remains ready for the next attack. Insecure intelligence is even sold on.

The victim gets their prized data back (hopefully) and vows never to get caught out again, really… $millions out of pocket to be back where they were originally and to stand still. Sadly, it does not end there. Much of the data may be compromised, and there are no guarantees that the data is not marked, or some kept for the next attack. It is reckoned only 8% of data in such cases is returned and not compromised.

Furthermore, who checks, and is able to check if there are a few SSL certificate plants expertly planted deep in the binaries of keystore whilst in there? The digital access doors that enabled, dare I say, even facilitated the infiltration in the first place are often left wide open for the next attack. Security is not improved or enhanced, and the losses written down and written off. If one were cynical, one could easily think this is a clever way to withdraw funds without any recourse and ultimately, the government and taxpayer pick up the tab.

Sadly, very few organisations seemingly really understand security or the root causes for being infiltrated in the first place. The Internet is always the best place to check first for security issues, as time after time, such suboptimal issues lead to being exposed, vulnerable, and exploited. It still amazes us that companies such as global leaders, regulators, and even governments do not understand the implications of being insecure at their public-facing and Internet connections or do not want to. The NSA and GCHQ perfected domain admin infiltration over twenty years ago, although clearly it was not in their interest to highlight the vulnerabilities. Even to this day, having first-hand experience of assisting both governments, they have begrudgingly accepted our research, and findings including the Central Voting System, the National Cyber Security Centre's (NCSC) own insecure domains, the FBI and No. 10 Downing Street.

In Autumn last year, uhnj.org (University Hospital of New Jersey) were in the middle of various crises, including COVID-19, and were victims of a Ransomware attack. They had certainly been remiss, having overlooked problems or even been guilty of basic security negligence by maintaining sub optimal and insecure domains, including the cardinal sin, their homepage, which relied upon an obsolete TLS cert. As such, their homepage lacked authentication and data integrity and was totally exposed to numerous known attacks, including hijacking, water holing, drive by, access, code injection, and, of course, plaintext data, the staple diet of Ransomware criminals. It seemingly proudly displayed the Not Secure text even after being informed and for several months.

We wrote to President and CEO Shereef Elnahal several times. Shereef is a highly revered and seemingly very well liked individual and expert in his field. We urged him to deal with the obsolete TLS issue over a period of six months. We even resorted to adding comments on his LinkedIn articles to gain his attention; nothing worked, and still today, UHNJ unbelievably remain Not Secure on their homepage, rendering the organisation, their patients' PII data, and connected third parties up- and downstream, exposed and vulnerable. Maintaining such a position is more than negligent; it is nothing short of gross incompetence and a major contributing factor to the sector's overall insecure position as well as the country's. Which part of NOT SECURE in the address bar do people not understand?

In May 2020, we alerted Alaska to their insecure position. Alaska was the first state of the fifty, and although we know Alabama is the first in the alphabetically listed states, a dear friend of mine Bob lives in Alaska, so by design we stared there. Following the research and very concerning findings including 27 CVEs, some critical and some dating back to 2011. We emailed and wrote several times to the Alaska government. Each message went unaddressed and ignored, even though they had suffered a PII Data breach the year before. On 4 December 2020, Alaska announced another breach, and once again, our research showed continued systemic lack of remediation and insecurity across the state's domains. This week, Alaska was breached again for a third time within two years. Our research shows Alaska's Court System maintaining a Not Secure homepage due again to an obsolete TLS. $millions, even $billions spent on resources, buildings, and infrastructure, yet Internet security is grossly overlooked and continually ignored; it should be made a criminal offense...

In a nutshell, Ransomware is one of the simplest of cyberattacks that are rarely touted as being 'Sophisticated', as companies are easily identified by cyber criminals for having easily exploited vulnerabilities along with plaintext data. Such attacks can take just hours to set running... Insurance companies do not help. Many insurance companies simply do not know what good cyber security looks like or what is required to prevent attacks. In fact, many, including some of the world's largest Insurers, such as Lloyd's of London, Aon, Willis, CNA, Zurich, and several more, are totally open to being breached themselves. One only has to look at CNA, who suffered a recent attack due to having sub optimal domain security, and also AXA, breached last week, ironically after declaring they will no longer guarantee Ransomware payments as part of a policy, then breached by, you guessed it, cyber criminals demanding a ransom... You could not make this stuff up, and when the CEO and Global CISO of AXA and Lloyd's of London refute the evidence of their insecure positions, it is little wonder. I thought Insurers were supposed to mitigate their clients' risks, not increase their risk, and yet the breaches at CNA and AXA make their clients more vulnerable, including the point of confirming policy details and thresholds of claims of Ransomware payments...

To be perfectly candid, many companies, Insurers, and governments are, without question, acting as their own worst enemies. A lack of knowledge and discipline is catching out company after company. Much of what we advocate is good basic security hygiene. Ignoring it, as Alaska have, CNA have, UHNJ have, and thousands of others who continue to ignore problems and act negligently have, is costing them and the global economy dearly. They will suffer multiple attacks and breaches until they finally either go out of business or start ensuring Internet, publicly facing, and connected security. It really is that simple.

As Steve Jobs said, there is no point hiring smart people and telling them what to do. In a very similar way, as one witnesses breach after breach and maintenance of the same insecure position, if you hire someone smarter, or more experienced people, please, stop and listen: use your ears and mouth in the ratio you have them. Equally, when you are alerted of vulnerabilities, just because you may not have requested it or paid for the actionable intelligence at that point, it most certainly does not mean its validity is any less impactful. Check first and then remediate. We also advocate rewarding such intelligence, as you would most certainly pay a bounty for bugs. Why might you refute or deny actionable intelligence as part of a Professional Disclosure that could prevent a full-blown breach that could cost hundreds of $millions?

As a Global CISO said to me yesterday of a $billion cyber security company, 'we scan daily, we have this, and that capability, I doubt you could show us anything, but I am prepared to listen'. Within hours we discovered a dozen totally insecure domains, rendering the company in the same position as SolarWinds were prior to being breached. With their government clients' highly sensitive data and connections, we were then ignored in what seems to be a personal reputational and egotistic situation and remains insecure to this day.

Ransomware and cyberattacks can be vastly reduced; however, we all need to work together to make the Internet and Internet connectivity safe. For every company, every organisation, every government, and every individual. Nowhere is that more important or critical than where it is connected to it...

4

COLONIAL PIPELINE AND CI COMPANIES

Over 6/7 May 2021, Colonial Pipeline, an American oil pipeline system that originates in Houston, Texas, and carries gasoline and jet fuel mainly to the Southeastern United States, suffered a Ransomware cyberattack. The attack did not impact the network that managed the pipeline and infrastructure, but the accounting for sales and invoicing. For a period of around a week, the pipeline was closed as gas stations ran out of fuel, which sparked something of a panic-buying situation. With reports of two-thirds of stations closed due to lack of fuel, it would not have taken much more to see a real panic and run-on fuel, or even criminal activity to source fuel.

On the evening of 6 May 2021, we undertook immediate research on www.colpipe.com Colonial's homepages, and discovered the usual array of F and 0 Ratings of domain security and several totally Not Secure domains. You will read this time after time throughout this book, when there are such Ratings of F and 0, it alerts cyber criminals that organisations are exposed, vulnerable, and easily exploited. Colonial had been, and remain, guilty of maintaining insecure domains, making themselves a target and then easily exploitable. The attack was neither sophisticated, nor were they originally a target; they encouraged that position by their own negligence. According to the *Wall Street Journal*, Colonial Pipeline Co.'s CEO, Joseph Blount, said that he authorised the payment of a $4.4 million ransom to DarkSide, the Ransomware attackers.

Colonial had apparently been trying to recruit security leadership for several weeks and had, and potentially still have, very limited security capability and knowledge. Given our research and findings, that may well be the case; however, having leadership and huge teams of security experts with massive budgets certainly does not mean that security is a given. As you will undoubtedly be shocked to see as you

DOI: 10.1201/9781003278214-4

read through this book and my previous book, *Stuxnet to Sunburst*, experience and expertise are no guarantee of security, no more than youth is a guarantee for innovation.

What has become clear—all too clear—is that we are living in a world of the Emperor's New Clothes to such an extent that cyber security firms and so-called security experts are guilty of not following good guidelines or best practice. Indeed, today, there is an article by *Infosecurity* magazine with the headline *Global CISOs Are Undermining Cyber-Hygiene Efforts* after a poll by Constella Intelligence. It revealed widespread poor security practices across the target group of over 100 Global CISOs, which is in keeping with our own research and findings. You will also see the words Complacent or Complicit appear frequently, as guidance and leadership must comply with good basic security and fit-for-purpose Internet connections, and yet from having conducted research, I would suggest over 75% of organisations have insecure positions. Of 1.2 billion websites, that is quite a target audience for cyber criminals to profit from...

As always, we are no strangers to looking at the bigger picture and were requested to research some of the US's top Critical Infrastructure fuel suppliers and to pull a report together for the well-respected group Energy Central. The research and article follow.

Is America's Critical National Infrastructure Prepared for the Ongoing Ransomware Siege, and What Can They Do to Avoid It?

The date is 30 December 2023, and this week, the US electric grid has been hit by two more devastating cyberattacks. Ransomware demands for a total of $200 million have been received as the grid is crippled for the fourth day in a row and several million people on the West Coast remain without power. The knock-on effect to stores, banks, communications, food storage, water treatment, and so on is mounting. Customers are outraged, as the public has demonstrated and attacked the homes of Executives of the Electric companies, with angry groups tearing down gates, walls, and defences. Sadly, sixteen people have died in one demonstration that got out of hand when law enforcement failed to manage the angry crowd, which resulted in crossfire, confusion, and a rampage. Investigations have started on the cause of these deaths; however probable stampeding by over fifty thousand angry customers is suspected to be the cause.

Anarchy has certainly fallen upon the West Coast and following last year's Ransomware attacks at the very same companies, their financial position may be that they are unable to meet the demands; it is unclear how this unbelievable situation will be resolved. In a damning report from last year, it has been revealed that Remote Access was gained through insecure Internet connections. Class action lawsuits of gross negligence have been filed by more than ten million customers who last year went without power for over a week, and over one hundred thousand people have had their digital identities stolen and misused, racking up debts for the totally innocent customers due to PII data theft. The White House and the President have issued an Executive Order, and the National Guard has been deployed, again.

This is the future the world currently faces, specifically the CI (Critical Infrastructure) providers, if they continue to ignore their Internet-facing and connected security...

Let us come back to today, 13 May 2021. This week we have witnessed the Colonial Pipeline cyberattack and breach that has caused a week of disruption. Gas stations and fuel lines have run dry, and a huge number of people on the East Coast are angry and want answers. The situation may only have been minimised by the restrictive effects of COVID-19. Fuel prices have escalated, and Colonial have been found not to have any security worthy of note, let alone good security or good security resources. This insecure position enabled and facilitated Remote Access, and in turn that Remote Access facilitated the breach. The total losses to Colonial this week, including the $millions Ransomware payment to Dark-Side, the Ransomware gang, may surpass $100 million. The overall security Rating of Colonial of F and 0 shows a worrying, systemic position:

> Colonial have a woeful Internet facing security Rating of F and 0. That is as bad as the ratings get and behind this rating lies a plethora of insecure, easily exploitable positions. Apart from being categorized as a CI, what has this to do with the Grid and its modernization?

The previous paragraph, dated 30 December 2023, is fast approaching, and as part of a research program we were asked by the CI Industry to undertake, the findings clearly indicate that unless the electric grid, RSO, and ISO companies add fit-for-purpose security as part of their programmes, they will fall victim to these attacks and be victims with all that will entail, including Class Action Lawsuits.

We were asked to research the security posture and Rating of the following providers within the sector, and the following findings should act as a major wakeup call and catalyst to drive change as part of the sector's overall plans before it is simply too late.

- PJM Interconnection
- MISO
- ERCOT
- SWPP
- NE ISO
- CAISO

PJM (PJM Interconnection LLC) is an RTO (regional transmission organisation) in the United States. It is part of the Eastern Interconnection grid operating an electric transmission system serving all or parts of Delaware, Illinois, Indiana, Kentucky, Maryland, Michigan, New Jersey, North Carolina, Ohio, Pennsylvania, Tennessee, Virginia, West Virginia, and the District of Columbia.

The Midcontinent Independent System Operator, Inc., formerly named MISO (Midwest Independent Transmission System Operator, Inc.), is an ISO (Independent System Operator) and regional transmission organisation providing open-access transmission service and monitoring the high-voltage transmission system in the Midwest United States; Manitoba, Canada; and a Southern United States region which includes much of Arkansas, Mississippi, and Louisiana. MISO also operates one of the world's largest real-time energy markets.

ERCOT (Electric Reliability Council of Texas, Inc.) is an American organisation that operates Texas's electrical grid, the Texas Interconnection, which supplies power to more than 25 million Texas customers and represents 90% of the state's electric load. ERCOT is the first independent system operator in the United States and one of nine ISOs in North America. ERCOT works with the TRE (Texas Reliability Entity), one of eight regional entities within the NERC (North American Electric Reliability Corporation) that coordinate to improve reliability of the bulk power grid.

SPP (Southwest Power Pool) manages the electric grid and wholesale power market for the central United States. As a regional transmission organisation, the non-profit corporation is mandated by the Federal Energy Regulatory Commission to ensure reliable supplies of power, adequate transmission infrastructure, and competitive wholesale electricity prices. Southwest Power Pool and its diverse group of member companies coordinate the flow of electricity across approximately 60,000 miles of high-voltage transmission lines spanning 14 states. The company is headquartered in Little Rock, Arkansas.

ISO-NE oversees the operation of New England's bulk electric power system and transmission lines, generated and transmitted by its member utilities, as well as Hydro-Québec, NB Power, the New York Power Authority, and utilities in New York state when the need arises. ISO-NE is responsible for reliably operating New England's 32,000-megawatt bulk electric power generation and transmission system. One of its major duties is to provide tariffs for the prices, terms, and conditions of the energy supply in New England. The Rating of B and 75/100 is a great improvement over others, and it would not be unreasonable to assume with this security Rating, ISO-NE would be the last CI on this list to be targeted.

CAISO (California Independent System Operator) is a non-profit independent system operator serving California. It oversees the operation of California's bulk electric power system, transmission lines, and electricity market generated and transmitted by its member utilities. The primary stated mission of CAISO is to 'operate the grid reliably and efficiently, provide fair and open transmission access, promote environmental stewardship, and facilitate effective markets and promote infrastructure development'. The CAISO is one of the largest ISOs in the world, delivering 300 million megawatt-hours of electricity each year and managing about 80% of California's electric flow.

The addition of a homepage demonstrating it is sub optimal and Not Secure in the address bar is in the security world a cardinal sin. By using obsolete TLS certificates, the organisation effectively renders the domain owner, the company, totally exposed to cyberattacks such as waterholes, drive-bys, shadow sites, lack of data integrity, and data stored as plaintext ready to be exfiltrated and encrypted as part of the Ransomware cycle.

Given the research and findings, and the fact that the security Ratings of all but one of these critical infrastructure organisations are sub optimal, many identical at F, the same Rating as Colonial, which has been shown to have been the root cause for the initial targeting and cyberattack, we can only hypothesise how many of these companies will fall foul of similar attacks and what disruption such attacks and subsequent outages might have. One thing for sure is Ransomware attacks have become big business. Cyber gangs do not care how much disruption they cause; in fact, the more the better, as it increases the likelihood of ransoms being paid more swiftly.

In conclusion, Colonial Pipeline and every organisation must take security seriously, and it cannot be by adding a cyber insurance policy, as the underwriters may deny any settlement if, like at Colonial, security was negligent and basic security was omitted. The previous picture is unequivocally dire and demonstrates a total lack of basic security across this sample group.

If the same intelligence were discovered by cyber criminals, I would seriously suspect that attacks were potentially already in flight. ... Finally, when is NOW a good time to address security? No matter what has gone before, security is the responsibility of every company and every Board Member and Executive, and the clock is ticking. Attacks on websites and servers are at the rate of 200,000 a day.

Playing Russian roulette (no pun intended) should not be a game of choice…

The previous article is due for publication within the next few weeks and yet may still result in plausible deniability and lack of action. We are of the firm belief that most breaches including Ransomware can be avoided. In the CI sector, any senior Executive or Board Members ignoring this critical area will find out the hard way and that with knock-on lessons for CI clients that will include Fuel and Energy, ultimately it may be a lights-out situation with major implications, including life-threatening situations.

Every company within the previous group was emailed, including several people in each. We have not yet, as of 21 May, one week later, received any responses…

5

CNA RANSOMWARE ATTACK AND CYBER INSURANCE

Commercial Insurance provider CNA Hardy were victims of a so-called sophisticated Ransomware attack on 21 March 2021 which impacted its operations, including emails and the network. Following the attack, the firm issued a statement regarding the online (a.k.a. Internet-connected) attack on its website. The website, its homepage, was sporting the Not Secure text on the address bar as well as others, and some quick research showed CNA's security Rating as F and 0. In fact having just checked, today, 21 May, the Rating has barely moved eight weeks later and sits at F and 10/100.

CNA commented that they immediately engaged a team of third-party forensic experts to investigate and determine the full scope of the incident. Rather a concern is why, then, two months later, are they still insecurely connected to the Internet where the original attack commenced? In fairness, that may be a tad harsh (however, not really), as last year's easyJet's breach 1 January 2020 saw a similar deployment of security experts and the NCSC before making the attack public in April 2020. We informed easyJet, along with their single largest shareholder and founder Stelios, that they were maintaining insecure domains along with sub optimal Not Secure domains that we believed where the root cause of the breach. For months and even to this day, easyJet.com are maintaining insecure domains with an F and 0 Rating over 12 months after going public and 16 months since they were breached. The Class Action Lawsuit for the massive 9 million customers who had their PII data exfiltrated is being pitched at £2000 per claimant, that is, a total of £18 billion. Our research and findings may find us working as expert witnesses and to evidence the gross negligence of basic security which clearly continues to this day.

Back in 2019, I was a guest at a major Cyber Insurance meeting in London's Mansion House hosted by AXA and Accenture. Both

DOI: 10.1201/9781003278214-5

companies were witnessing major changes and uptake on Cyber Insurance. I spoke to Partners of Accenture on the trial we had performed for them in Germany with their head of PKI and the Country leading Partner. We used Whitethorn to scan their Gold Standard newly prepared laptop. The findings were shocking and effectively showed them that they could lose C2 (Command and Control) at any time. One of the plethora of adverse findings were several Chinese Digital certificates (CNNIC) with full Admin Access (like SolarWinds) but with validity for 999 years. This is a major Red Flag and shocked the team; however, it was played down months later even though the German team were literally in shock at the findings on their own controlled laptop.

In the meeting at Mansion House, I spoke with AXA's CEO re understanding exactly what they were insuring and how it would be extremely beneficial to get visibility of exactly what was embedded within the devices, network and facing to, and connected with the Internet. I also spoke to the Accenture Partners on the findings and agreed to further discussions. The consensus was, of course, if we know what we are dealing with by gaining visibility, we can control, manage, and secure it. At the time, we naively thought we were going to make a major impact in the world of security and finally let security and security products do their jobs by not being undermined by rogue certificates and insecure Internet-connected domains. Our naïveté turned to a degree of frustration as AXA and indeed Accenture's global CISO, Kelly Bissell decided their PKI anomalies were of no consequence. ... In other words, what is placed (planted) within their systems to enable and facilitate backdoors and harvesting was not of interest to them. In hindsight, of course, we now fully understand that governments and agencies are working with these companies with access and capabilities that are not discussed openly. Do as you are told and ask no questions. As such, the Cyber Insurance market and Accenture, possibly the world's largest cyber security provider, only have fractional security capability and knowledge. The $billions being invoiced to provide security are limited and fractional and just like today's global condemnation of the BBC's Panorama's handling of the Princess Diana interviews, deception, and manipulation, the 900 families wrongly convicted of theft by the UK's Post Office due to Fujitsu's faulty technology, or the ongoing lawsuits against Du Pont for lethal Tefal implications and premature deaths for many years, smoke, mirrors and revenues are all important, not doing the right thing. In 2021, Accenture suffered a major cyberattack, now there's a surprise.

Governments and agencies DO NOT want organisations to have proper security, only fractional security at best. The backdoors and insecure positions are not only welcomed by them, but they are also actively inserted and enforced.

Back to Cyber Insurance, which has been actively encouraged and is now considered a must have and a highly desirable option as part of the overall strategy for organisations who face business interruption, disruption, system replacements, and lost revenues due to nefarious cyberattacks. However, should it not follow and be a given that Insurers themselves, as well as their clients, have strong cyber resilience and basic security in place? Such a situation would ensure Best Practice and enable benchmarking of fit-for-purpose security along with evidence demonstrating what 'good' actually looks like? Customers take cyber cover in their attempt to provide additional risk mitigation; they do not expect a breach to originate via their cyber insurance provider, and yet the CNA breach is proving just that…

The world's leading Insurers collectively underwrite policies that could be liable to settled claims totalling $billions and ensure the stabilisation, post breach, of thousands of employees. Is it not therefore imperative that all parties, the Insurer, and the Insured, adopt and are able to demonstrate the very strongest and most resilient cyber posture and maintain such a position throughout the lifespan of the policy? Sadly, this is not the case, in fact, it is rarely ever the case.

There is much controversy currently over Insurers enabling and settling payments on claims against Ransomware attacks. Earlier this year, the former head of the NCSC, Ciaran Martin, said, 'Insurers paying ransomware demands were fuelling cybercrime'. I agree with Mr Martin; however, I do not agree with the lack of NCSC and Insurer action within this and other sectors. Writing a cautionary note to be included in one's handbook is hardly taking all-out action. It certainly is not taking the urgently required proactive stance on cyberattack prevention or the greatly needed increase in security posture. Don't forget, the NCSC are in all UK companies that suffer breaches, yet months later, the company still display woeful Internet security, hardly thought leading and progress…

In real terms, the Cyber Insurance sector is still in its infancy. Yet the sector is making some huge, extremely influential decisions that are having an incredible impact. Sadly, mistakes are also being made. Let me explain. Insurance Actuaries are scrambling and desperate for data and metrics within the cyber world to base their models of probability on within this immature new market. Furthermore, because of the lack of cyber security knowledge, from a defensive and indeed offensive standpoint, as well as what maintaining good basic cyber security really looks like and means, they are themselves made prime targets with little to no defence, as CNA and others have found out to their great cost.

Last weekend, AXA made a statement that they would no longer guarantee Ransomware settlements as part of a cyber insurance policy. Our research in which we continuously look at majors such as AXA had their Internet security rated very poor, and within a week of making their bold statement, AXA were made the victim of a Ransomware cyberattack; just like CNA and others, their Internet connectivity is acting like beacons, easily identifiable for cyber gangs to identify, see where the vulnerabilities are, and launch attacks.

Let us look more closely at CNA: unquestionably a major Insurance company and yet so easily breached whilst at the same time lacking basic security, as can be seen by the Not Secure text on their address bar. As of today, I can confirm the homepage, www.cna.com, is now secure; however, other subdomains of CNA's remain insecure. CNA remain vulnerable and exposed to being further exploited. To confirm, CNA are as vulnerable today as the day they were initially breached and, through a lack of knowledge, incorrectly believe they are secure by virtue of their homepage, whereas in truth, all of their Internet-facing domains and subdomains are still insecure and further exploitable. Not to mention what infiltration and Plants may have occurred for later use.

Another major concern has been inadvertently created whereby many organisations, as part of their cyber strategy, purchase cyber insurance only to incorrectly consider the policy a 'get out of jail free card' and by default, sometimes even by design, overlook or even ignore the basics, as they unquestionably should not. All too often, insuring parties complete policy document forms with little more than a tick box, subjective exercise to evaluate a policy and premium.

The fact that both parties may be falling foul of good security and potentially by doing so breaching United Kingdom Data Protection Act (UKDPA), GDPR, and local Privacy laws on data security and PII data protection is also being overlooked. Both parties may be maintaining poor cyber security but demonstrating real depth and knowledge to the market. It does not take too much imagination to realise why one could see things move from bad to worse very rapidly. There are several legal cases currently whereby the Insured party have not had a claim settled due to ambiguities—that and/or a claim of an 'Act of War'.

The problem goes much deeper, as the Insurance companies seemingly do not fully comprehend, understand, or adhere to good cyber security practices themselves, and nowhere is that more important than at that the critical Internet-facing and connected websites they are supposed to maintain and, like it or not, are responsible for. No one would ever maintain such a position if they fully comprehended the risk and exposure, would they?

AON is a multinational British professional services firm that sells a range of financial risk-mitigation products, including insurance, pension administration, and health-insurance products. They employ approximately 50,000 employees in some 120 countries. They have revenues of over $10 billion and are among the world's leading Insurance companies. In March 2020, AON moved to buy Willis in what was the world's largest insurance deal. The deal was for nearly $30 billion and would have created the world's largest Insurance broker. The combined value of Aon and Willis would be around $80 billion.

As part of a program, we researched leading Insurers globally. Both AON and Willis were clearly maintaining very concerning and unacceptable Security Ratings of F and 0/100 and 10/100, respectively. In other words, Internet-facing security could not be any worse and has been maintained in this position for some time. This places AON in a highly vulnerable and exploitable position, as well as their investors and customers. On the back of our research and findings, an article was written by the esteemed Cyber Insurance journalist Mia Wallace, the UK National Editor of Insurance Business and Key Media, which covered the systemic lack of security across several major players in the space, including Lloyd's of London, AON, Willis, CNA, Zurich, and others.

Many markets, including the Insurance market, are unquestionably attractive hunting grounds for cyber criminals. First, they hold a lot of sensitive client data, data the Insurers and their clients would rather not want exposed or exploited. Second, they are clearly major organisations with matching turnovers, profits, and values. Lastly, it is clearly bad form to be caught out as a Cyber Insurer, for example, to be successfully attacked with Ransomware and breached. There is a perverse satisfaction for many criminals to beat the Insurers at their own game, especially AXA after their previous announcement. Cyber criminals are looking for and targeting companies that maintain insecure Internet-facing and connected positions. As part of criminals' nefarious reconnaissance, they can ascertain the cyber cover and the provider once they have infiltrated the organisation such as they have at CNA. It has become a known fact that cyber criminals are targeting organisations with cyber insurance policies. ... The sad fact of the matter is most Insurers, including those providing cyber insurance, are allowing themselves to be sitting ducks playing with their, and their clients', security posture. The situation is more akin to being at a blackjack table in Las Vegas than encouraging and enforcing improved cyber resilience and the prevention of successful attacks as supposed professional experts in their field.

Zurich Insurance Group is a Swiss insurance company based in Zurich. It is Switzerland's largest Insurer and was founded in 1872. As of 2020, Zurich was named the world's 117th largest company with revenues of over $40 billion. It employs over 55,000 people and is in 215 countries around the globe. Zurich is currently in a legal battle with Mondelez, who are suing Zurich for their NotPetya attack in 2019, which saw 1,700 servers and 24,000 laptops affected as the Not-Petya Ransomware swept through its Network and systems. When Mondelez originally claimed against their policy, Zurich made an offer that was initially rejected and then retracted. Zurich has stated that the NotPetya virus constitutes an Act of War, and the policy does not cover such acts.

I am unsure how much more the Cyber Insurance sector needs to mature and gain data for their Actuaries to provide better intelligence; however, I would suggest the Actuaries certainly are being thrown curve balls by using the data collected so far. It certainly should not be aligned with their own errors, breaches, losses, and costs. There is a much simpler and better way. Just as the world's Financial Markets depend upon Credit Rating Agencies, why do the insurance and other markets not have a reliable Secure Rating facility? Such a solution would enable evidence-based policies, vastly improved security postures, and a reduction in attacks. We have designed and offered such a solution that would provide a unique insight and capability, plus vastly improved knowledge and understanding.

Why might any individual or company not want to know the security posture and Rating of a company they were looking to do business with? It does not matter if it is a multi-$billion M&A deal, an IPO, or a cyber insurance policy for $50 million. If you do not have a clearly evidenced security posture, it may not be too long before you wish you had. Insurers could, for the first time, provide much of the lacking expertise and basic security by design instead of playing a 'numbers game'.

If we have learned anything from the recent SolarWinds breach, the Microsoft breach CVE-2021-26855, or indeed the breach at CNA, it is they all suffered initial access that was related to, and because of, insecure SSL/TLS digital certificates and websites. All the examples in our research and reports show this. Such situations, with the right tools and capability, are in the public domain and yet continually overlooked, ignored, and left to chance. Insurance companies need to become more security savvy; currently, this is clearly not the case.

Lloyd's of London, simply known as Lloyd's, is the world's leading insurance and reinsurance marketplace. Lloyd's was set up in 1686 by Edward Lloyd. As of 2019, Lloyd's has 80 syndicates managed by 54 agencies that collectively wrote £35.9 billion of gross premiums. Unlike most of its competitors in the Industry, Lloyd's is not an insurance company; rather, Lloyd's is a corporate body governed by the Lloyd's Act of 1871 and subsequent Acts of Parliament. Lloyd's in many ways is considered the 'voice' of all global insurance and a leader within the new world of Cyber Insurance. Sadly, Lloyd's themselves are as guilty as those already mentioned in the Insurance market when it comes to security, as evidenced by maintaining sub optimal, highly vulnerable, and easily exploitable websites with a Rating of F and a score of 0. One only must consider last year's Blackbaud or Solar-Winds breaches to understand a single breach can force thousands of subsequent breaches.

Last year we 'assisted' Hiscox who, like most Insurers, seemingly did not have the governance, control, or management of their Internet-facing domains when, rather embarrassingly and rather ironically, we alerted them to the fact their Cyber Insurance website was Not Secure: its TLS certificate was invalid. Few people relish being technically challenged, or their errors being pointed out, this situation was no exception. After what bizarrely became a rather heated debate, the CISO and CEO finally relented and made their cyber and data insurance site secure by placing a valid certificate on the domain. There was barely a thank you; possibly they preferred the alternative. Their security position to date is still far from ideal.

All the while organisations, especially Insurance companies, that provide cyber cover continue to overlook, ignore, or are complacent with their Internet-facing and connected security, cyberattacks, losses, and even companies ceasing to trade will exponentially increase. In 2021, cybercrime will become equivalent to the world's third-largest economy, with total estimated costs and losses of $6–7 trillion (circa 10% of the world's entire GDP). By 2025, that figure is estimated to surpass $10 trillion.

The insurance market has a vital part to play. By seemingly supporting and dare I say inadvertently encouraging inadequate basic security, it is fuelling a potential for even greater losses. It is time to insist on the equivalent of '5 lever latches, window locks' and alarms before it is simply too late. Being complicit by being complacent is sadly all too frequent a position, as our reports continually evidence.

Finally, ask yourself this simple question, no matter if you are in the Insurance sector or not. If you drove your car whilst drunk, without papers, with four illegal tyres, and recklessly, or if you left your property for a year, with the windows and doors left wide open and all your valuable possessions on the table in full view, if you were then in an accident or were robbed, would you expect an insurance claim and settlement? Of course not; so why do organisations (including Insurers themselves) demonstrate such a poor stance on basic security measures year after year and then have the gall to call attacks 'sophisticated' when they were nothing more than opportunistic with regard to exploitable vulnerabilities? What is more, these cyberattack opportunities have red carpeted runways and being served up on silver platters…

Security Ratings will cause a marked reduction and huge difference in day-to-day security. To decrease cyberattacks and losses, changes must be driven, even enforced. Sadly, I am unsure what, if any, real changes governments and agencies really want or are prepared to sacrifice.

As of today, 21 May, it has been reported by Bloomberg that CNA paid $40 million two weeks after the initial cyberattack and that data had been exfiltrated. This meant plaintext data, the staple diet of all cyber criminals, was removed and then encrypted. As in typical Ransomware fashion, the decryption key is what ransoms are paid for to obtain. Previous research we had undertaken during the original attack was checked late last night, and CNA are maintaining their insecure Internet connectivity and Not Secure domains due to obsolete SSL certificates.

The fact the original cyberattack was not classed as a Ransomware attack, then was, with a small ransom payment, and now the disclosure of the $40 million calls into question exactly what is being said. The Colonial ransom payment has been claimed to be $4.4 million by the company; however, sources have alluded to the $30-million demand being met.

The question remains: at what point do the NSA, GCHQ, FBI, NCSC, and United States and United Kingdom governments finally do something other than play charades with these attacks? Forget the fact they have been guilty of Internet abuse and manipulation for mass data collection and harvesting for over two decades; they hold the key to confirming that lacking Internet security is the main cause, the root cause, for $trillions of losses due to cybercrime. What motive could they possibly have to continue playing this down, or do they have a patent on the word 'sophisticated'?

6
BA, easyJet, and the Travel Industry

Long before COVID-19 was even thought about, well at least to the majority of the world's population, back in August 2018, customers of British Airways were merrily booking their flights to far-flung and exotic places. It was not until sometime later that they realised 1) they were going nowhere, and 2) they had booked flights on a Shadow website due to a series of basic security oversights at BA.

Due to BA's lack of Internet security controls and management, cyber criminals 'stood up' a spoof website called BAWays.com that was in essence a carbon copy of BA's own website. It emulated all the functions and allowed bookings and, importantly, the collection of PII data and payment. To cut a long story short, BA were found guilty by the ICO of negligence to secure and protect their customers data due to said basic security failings. The ICO originally levied a fine of £183 million which, due to the economic challenges and COVID-19, was greatly reduced to £20 million. BA then initially borrowed £500 million increasing to some £2 billion from the government backed by the British taxpayer. It is still unclear if BA have actually paid the reduced fine. The ICO said at the time: 'When organisations make poor decisions around people's personal data, that can have a real impact on people's lives. The law now gives us the tools to encourage businesses to make better decisions about data, including investing in up-to-date security' (Elizabeth Denham, Commissioner ICO). BA were fined 1% of the money they borrowed, sounds about right...

The original fine was calculated on the GDPR regulations of enabling a fine up to 4% of BA's annual revenues; however, as the fine levied from the time of the incident was over two years, that was frowned upon by Industry experts. The ICO said it 'meant business' and is not letting struggling companies off the hook for their data protection failures.

DOI: 10.1201/9781003278214-6

Quick research today confirms that British Airways have clearly not learnt much from the breach and have seemingly taken absolutely no action whatsoever so far as improving their security, which in turn means no additional security measures for their customers. With a Rating of an F and a score of 0 out of 100 yesterday, it is fair to say BA's homepage, and their customers, could not be more vulnerable or exploitable. Maybe if we were to use the Cyber Analysis Rating, as previously suggested, further fines could be levied unless the firm complies with basic security measures. If you have several illegal issues with your car, you cannot barter for a 'collective' deal; equally, if you got stopped several months later with the same issues, would you expect leniency because you had paid a fine? Of course not, so why are BA and hundreds, if not thousands of, other companies addressing breaches and fines as a cost of doing business but ignoring making any improvements? That is simply madness.

We decided to look at other Airlines to see if this was a one-off over-sight or if lacking security were as systemic as it is in other sectors. In April 2020, easyJet, with support from the NCSC, announced easy-Jet had been breached three months earlier in January; however, they decided they would delay informing the public. Personally Identifiable Information data of some nine million customers was stolen, making it a substantial attack. It was also termed the usual 'sophisticated attack'. We researched easyJet extensively and found a plethora of insecure domains and F- and 0-rated homepages. Furthermore, when easyJet made the public announcement, just like Travelex did, the website on which they made the public apology and update was a Not Secure domain. You could not make this up. There in black and white was the text Not Secure in front of easyJet. The certificate was invalid, and they were now letting the entire world know; however, what it confirmed is that they themselves were ignorant of domain management and security, as was their audi-ence. It took us weeks and weeks to even get them to listen.

The screenshots we took, and hold confirmed basic security was not in place during the initial breach. That rendered the easyJet domains Not Secure, exposed, vulnerable, and easily exploited. Many of these screenshots have not altered, and many easyJet domains remain woe-fully insecure. But hey, oversight and errors can occur, right? So today when we look at the easyJet homepage, it is all good, right? Well, sadly, no, it is not. With the same Rating, F, and score, 0, as BA, easyJet are not addressing or improving the protection of the company or, more importantly, their customers, and the current vulnerabilities can easily be further exploited. Surely this is just an unfortunate coincidence: the wider Industry has witnessed these lessons and have learnt from them; I hear you cry?

We have been asked to act as expert witnesses in several cases to evidence security failings and provide hard evidence of the same. As a Security professional, it grates on me that so-called security experts simply do not do what they know or should know and then overlook, forget, or ignore the basics. I have been known to say on many occasions that it is far simpler to prove security negligence than it is to get a company to listen to sound advice and take basic security measures. It makes no sense whatsoever to leave such exposure. Once again, it begs the question, complacent or complicit? Security professionals should not compromise the basics; if they are asked to ignore the basics or leave the business exposed, they should be strong enough and confident enough, let alone experienced enough, to refrain from doing so and ensure the basics are done. Any failure to do so is a mark on their ability and character.

In the first week of March 2021, just several weeks ago, SITA (Star Alliance) suffered a cyberattack which affected numerous other airlines. Again, this attack was also termed Sophisticated, which is for two main reasons. 1) it sounds a lot better than 'we left the digital doors wide open and totally ignored basic security', and 2) Insurance companies and Regulators seem to be more lenient when the term 'Sophisticated' is used. ... You will never hear the following no matter how true it is: 'We were negligent and complacent; we simply did not do our jobs properly'.

The Travel Industry in the United Kingdom in 2019 saw 93.1 million visits overseas, meaning 93.1 million people completed PII data forms and trusted the travel providers to ensure that data was secure. Many countries and companies are totally reliant upon tourism; however, like the row of dominos or the house built of cards, they can tumble one by one or all at once. The Travel Industry, like Healthcare, MNOs (Mobile Network Operators), and many others, simply do not have anywhere near enough focus, or skill so far as security is concerned and yet are targeted day in day out and maintain insecure positions. It is simply inevitable that breaches will occur.

We then looked at Malaysia Air, who were breached in March 2010 and remained totally exposed until June 2019. With our recent research and findings, we would suggest they still are very much exposed. You may notice a common theme of F Ratings and 0 scores for airlines' Internet-facing homepages. These are the websites tens if not hundreds of millions of customers land on that are clearly frequently targeted successfully to launch attacks such as Shadow sites, water hole attacks, man in the middle, or even domain takeover. What is clear is that the companies themselves are guilty of not taking security seriously, and all the time the taxpayers bail them out: so, what? The fine from the ICO was ultimately pathetic and set the trend for what we witness constantly, which is systemic insecure positions, rendering the airlines insecure and breaching all data privacy acts. I am hopeful the Class Action Lawsuits will hold these organisations to account and responsible for their negligence. I would urge the Civil Aviation Authority to launch investigations into the lack of security as well as the wider Aviation Authorities. They may wish to address their own also, as their homepage has serious security vulnerabilities.

What is deeply disturbing is: at what point will an Executive Order or the NCSC stop the charade and start encouraging companies to realise the critical importance of taking security of their Internet connectivity seriously, as opposed to simply having it manipulated? When a company such as UK Tech, UK Finance, and Critical National Infrastructure/nuclear power organisations ignore our Actionable Intelligence with evidence of insecurity, Chinese and Russian infiltration because GCHQ suggested it did not matter, something is seriously wrong. For the avoidance of all doubt, our goal, that is, as an individual and as an organisation, is to make companies more secure and to address the grossly overlooked insecurity of thousands of companies, companies that are being breached day after day. I guess the NSA's and GCHQ's goals must differ from ours; there certainly seems to be a major disparity.

Maybe taxpayers need to lend more money to the airlines and spend more on the agencies so they can address security...

7

DESTABILISING THE UNITED STATES, COURTS, LAW ENFORCEMENT, AND WAY OF LIFE

What has become all too obvious over the last decade or so, and even more so in the last few years, is that due to the Internet being abused and misused to gather and harvest data, actions that often bordered on illegal activity and using various methods, the very same methods to collect that data, can be and have been used to attack the very people who use it to trade, shop, communicate, and so on online. Data has become the world's most valuable commodity, and that does not matter if you are using it, trawling it, capitalising upon it, harvesting it, manipulating it, or charged with securing it.

This month's Ransomware attack and subsequent closure of Colonial Pipeline's fuel distribution and infrastructure poses a serious question about what economic damage might be caused if a cyberattack rendered the Internet unusable for say, an hour, ten hours, or a day. The company, Merchant Machine, a UK-based payment information service, took a stab at estimating a figure for the economic damage that the loss of the Internet could create. The figures that they came up with are as follows: The world economy would lose $2.1 billion per hour—rising to $51 billion after 24 hours. It naturally would follow that the larger the country's economy, the larger the loss. Therefore, the US economy would be on a $306.3 million an hour loss rate, or $7.3 billion after 24 hours. China would lose about $244 million per hour, or $5.8 billion after 24 hours. So, when the Biden Administration says it is ploughing an additional $500 million into cyber security, that is only the equivalent to preventing a US total outage of an hour and a half in real term losses.

Recently the City of Tulsa was the latest victim of a Ransomware attack. This attack followed many other similar attacks on Cities in the

DOI: 10.1201/9781003278214-7

United States that also fell 'victim' to Ransomware attacks. Atlanta, Baltimore, Denver, Knoxville, New Orleans, and Alaska for a third time all fell victim to cyberattacks, and all have incurred massive costs in addition to ransom payments. In July 2019, the US Conference of Mayors unanimously passed a resolution calling on local officials to stop paying Ransomware demands to cybercriminal gangs who were infiltrating and taking over their Networks. However, despite that resolution, many Cities have paid huge ransom demands after being faced with the extortion or exposure of highly sensitive and important data and after being threatened with the data being made inaccessible or publicly available. Addressing the symptoms rather than the cause seems to be a favourite pastime.

We researched many of the States, Tulsa being the most recent, and found a plethora of outdated technical systems, countless CVEs, along with insecure domains connected to the Internet. Even if we spent weeks forensically pinpointing the access point, that would be seriously hampered by the sheer number of accessible and easily infiltrated access points. So bad is the Network and Internet-connected security of local governments that the easily accessible entry points would make the task near impossible. Furthermore, Tulsa is far from a one-off; it is a systemic issue and national tale of insecurity across many States and includes the US government itself. It was only a few months ago that we notified the White House and the then-President of the United States, Donald J. Trump, that both had insecure domains. Donald Trump had several, in fact, as part of his digital re-election campaign and was collecting donations (and PII Data) on totally Not Secure domains. This was poor form and broke numerous Privacy laws and regulations on the collection of said PII data. Both positions and numerous insecure domains still exist. Hardly surprising, some of Donald J. Trump's domains suffered cyberattacks, taking the domains offline for a day.

Websites are simply not a fit and forget; they need controls and constant management, or they will bite, and bite hard. In most cases, from Amazon through to the White House, from a SolarWinds to Blackbaud or Codecov, organisations get online and simply take a flyer; they rarely ensure their websites are secure, even sometimes from the word go. Certainly, the majority of legacy websites are overlooked, forgotten, neglected, or ignored. Then hacked.

The very fabric of America and indeed the US democracy is being torn to shreds, and instead of the agencies and government providing the technology and expertise and driving a planet-scale change, they are throwing $billions at their ex-colleagues, many of whom now run security firms with $billion contracts with the government, who ultimately are little more secure than they were before. In fact, many of the security firms themselves perversely increase the exposure and vulnerability because they themselves are insecure and by default add to their client's security woes. Good old Bob with a 25-year agency track record, no due diligence gets the outsourced contract...

The same tactics, tools, and methods they have used and repurposed for years are simply not working. All the time governments and agencies spend (waste) on doing the same thing over and over is not preventing any cyberattacks, quite literally the opposite. Two weeks ago, we sent intelligence via a very well-known third party to the attention of Paul Nakasone. It showed a plethora of US government websites that were totally exposed and using obsolete TLS certificates. Remember this is how SolarWinds, the world's most devastating breach to a single organisation, occurred when they had a domain hijacking and takeover which then provided Domain Admin Access. One such situation was the Committee on National Security Systems, quite an important committee without question. Here was their homepage, complete with login credentials, using an obsolete TLS certificate and displaying the Not Secure text in the address bar. What made this all even more worrying, but none the less ironic, is this committee and this domain is where National Security groups go to get digital certificates and their PKI directives, instructions, operational procedures, and so on. There, as clear as day, sat the keys to the American Intelligence Kingdom, and it is Not Secure. Several weeks later, we never heard back from Paul Nakasone or his office. A further several weeks later, however, I am pleased to see the sites we alerted them to have been removed. A polite thank you would not be too much to expect, just like the FBI when we discovered and assisted them with the Korean DNS in Central Voting. Is this arrogance, embarrassment, or egos? Possibly a combination of all three.

'We are on the cusp of a Global Pandemic', Christopher Krebs said recently. As the first Director of the CISA (Cybersecurity and Infrastructure Security Agency), Christopher is a well-liked, respected, and acknowledged as an expert in his field. He went on to say; 'The virus causing the Pandemic wasn't biological, it was software'. What Christopher, and sadly all his colleagues, fail to acknowledge, or impart upon the Senate, the American public, Captains of Industry, or even those at the coalface tasked with trying to secure Corporate America, is that their insecure connectivity is causing the freefall the United States and the rest of the world are experiencing. With losses, as mentioned previously, surpassing $6 trillion in 2021, when will the time come to comprehend this incredible faux pas, this ridiculous, totally frustrating, and unnecessary position? What ulterior motive, other than keeping face, could there be? US states, major cyber security firms, state law courts, Critical National Infrastructure fuel companies, energy companies, and even law enforcement organisations are becoming victims of cyberattacks and breaches daily. The EO does not even mention insecure websites and domains that provide total unfettered access to the very heart of Corporate America. I thought the smell of coffee was loved in the United States; it's time to start smelling it.

Talking of State Courts being attacked, it was only a few weeks ago that Alaska Court notified the public that they had been the target of a cyberattack. Alaska, you may recall, was the first of the 50 States we researched for Internet security last year. We attempted to notify the Alaskan government at the time and subsequently the Court that were hacked had been due to them having woeful Internet-connected security, which was accompanied by a screenshot of courts.alaska.gov with an apology note for services being down due to a cyberattack. The homepage, rather reminiscent of easyJet, Travelex, and countless others, was served on a Not Secure homepage. … Once again, a major error (possibly that bloody intern moonlighting from SolarWinds again) confirming to the world that no controls or management of Internet security was in place. As such, it was open season to have a go as attacks rained down. Alaska has been attacked no less than three times in the last two years, and ever since we started research on Alaska, they have been content to remain insecure and seemingly taken no action to better secure their position. Maybe someone is simply being complicit?

We have discussions after discussions with organisation after organisation in this area. Sometimes it is post breach; other times it is to be proactive to prevent breaches. The one thing that remains constant is that we typically witness a lack of knowledge and understanding of their current insecure position, what can be achieved via their insecurity, and what access can be gained by maintaining insecure domains. It should never be about egos or matters of opinion. If we alert a company, be it SolarWinds, Colonial, Codecov, Boeing, Committee on National Security Systems (CNSS), or even Alaska Courts, it does not require a debate or differing subjective opinions. There is an exposed, unacceptable vulnerability, and if (when) exploited, the organisation will more than likely suffer a major breach.

Last year the NCSC were very nearly agreeing with our thoughts and said they have 'Webchecker' for that very reason and that they offer it as a free service to companies. It was at that point I shared a redacted, highly sensitive report showing a plethora of CVEs and obsolete TLS certificates. The Technical Director, Dr Ian Levy, agreed it certainly required further investigation and could not disagree with me that no company should never place themselves in such a position. It was why they relied upon Webchecker. At that point, I informed him the report was an NCSC subdomain report that was Not Secure. He asked for further information, including the IP address...

We know that it can be hard to manage all domains and subdomains; we acknowledge that it requires discipline and constant, daily management to avoid being made a target, directly or indirectly, by third-party content, a planted cookie, a water hole, or a drive-by or code injection attack. However, trust me when I say it is a lot easier to ensure this is done regularly than the alternative of being a victim of a cyberattack and then trying to pretend it was sophisticated. I have to question what the government actually really wants to achieve. We know of numerous cyberattacks in which the government has been called into due to the sensitivity and CNI position, and yet over a year later, the organisation is just as exposed as the day they were hacked and exposed to being further attacked at their perimeter (domains) due to continued oversight and ignorance but are taking advice from the NCSC and leading expert. EasyJet and the MNO Three spring to mind; there are literally hundreds of more examples. If I were on the outside looking in, I would seriously consider it was the desired outcome. If the company has been negligent, that is one thing; however, then to call one of the Big 4 and/or the NCSC and remain exposed and exploitable, surely is gross negligence and complicit? With all the expertise and advice from these 'Trusted' organisations, leaders, and experts surely cannot be anything other than by design?

On 11 May 2021, a Ransomware group known as Babuk leaked internal files from the Washington Police Department (MPDC) from a cyberattack and ransom demand in late April the month before. The data released included PII data of both officers and criminals, and their Social Security numbers, credit history, addresses, and contact details. In addition, the leaked documents included polygraph tests, social media posts, employment history, financial liabilities, and copies of officers' driving licences. Negotiations had broken down between Babuk and the MPDC. Being a Law Enforcement Department, it was decided paying a Ransomware demand was not befitting the organisation, which is perfectly correct, especially knowing that any ransoms paid would fuel further criminal activities; the term 'Own Goal' springs to mind. The FBI were quoted at the time as saying: 'We do not support paying any ransom as payment does not guarantee any organisation would receive their data back'. It would also be seen as encouraging adversaries to target more victims and increase overall cyberattacks and Ransomware. The FBI suffered their own digital intrusion in November 2021 when 100,000 FBI emails were sent to unsuspecting recipients. The emails certainly came from the FBI servers, just not sent by anyone in the FBI. The FBI had lost Command and Control of their own servers (Mail Exchange (MX)) due to maintaining Insecure subdomains that were hacked.

Once again, we launched our own research and investigation into the MPDC's Internet security and immediately found a sub optimal Rating of F and 0 (very nearly the title of this book: F0) and alerted the department accordingly. At the same time, we wanted to understand why such a situation had been allowed to manifest itself and why they lacked the ongoing control and management that any Law Enforcement Department should have. Why would the MPDC leave their departmental doors open, systems logged in, and unrestricted total free and unrestricted access? Of course, they should not, yet that is exactly what they had done via their easily exploited insecure Internet connections. We wanted to research and look further. We added other major Law Enforcement Departments including the NYPD, LAPD, Chicago, Philadelphia, Houston, Cook County, LA County, Pennsylvania, and Dallas Law Enforcement Departmental domains. All, apart from Chicago, who scored a D+ and 40/100, still far from an A Rating, had woeful Ratings of F. ... That meant all these Law Enforcement Departments had the same, totally exposed, vulnerable, and exploitable position as the already breached Washington Police Department, America's Federal Capital Department. Be afraid, be very afraid. In December 2021, the Police UK Police National Computer (PNC) was hacked and the data of 13 million UK people, mainly criminals or certainly within the criminal system. The hack was blamed on an earlier attack at NDItech, a UK technology company who boast they look after a large percentage of the PNC. In October 2021, they had themselves been hacked due to suboptimal basic security and Police UK pointed the finger at them. When we supplied reports to the Chief Commissioner and the Home Secretary after being requested as experts to look at the City of London Police's website security, they had closed some down, the reports were so damning that we were marginalised, ostracised, and ignored. These reports will be made public soon.

The above situations are incredibly damning and must be a major concern for every US Senator, Mayor, Police Officer, and indeed Citizen. For the country's Capital Police Department to be so easily attacked and data exfiltrated shows just how poor security is and, given our research, must act as a warning of things to come. When Law Enforcement, Country Courts, the US government, and even the US Treasury can be breached, it shows the systemic failing of the government and each department to secure their data and enable day-to-day business to be conducted. As I have mentioned before, the Biden Administration have this week announced a further $500 million to be allocated to cybercrime; however, one cannot help but wonder who the criminals really are. One thing for sure, when, and if the dust settles and the grey suits start legal proceedings and Class Action Lawsuits for gross negligence against these organisations, the Cyber companies with their backing and orders from the US government, mostly led by ex-Agency staff and many invested in by Thoma Bravo and others, will more than likely continue banking vast sums of monies but frequently failing to offer any additional security. In fact, many are increasing the exposure of their clients. Thoma Bravo are major investors in several very high-profile Cyber Companies that all have been breached in the last two years. Am I cynical? Not by nature. Am I trusting? I certainly was until the last several years. Am I disappointed with the government and their Intelligence Agencies? I am, unequivocally disgusted.

When I was 'selected' and invited to be the CEO of Cybersec Innovation Partners, I thought, no problem, we take on the bad guys; I have broad shoulders, am smart and very streetwise. I never thought for one minute that the so-called good guys would soon thereafter want to literally blindfold me and metaphorically tie my hands behind my back. I did not stop to think for a moment that when we discovered Russian and Chinese presence and infiltration in UK-based Critical National Infrastructure along with a plethora of revoked, expired, illegal, and sanctioned digital certificates, they would tell the Board to ignore the findings as if they had never happened. Likewise, I never thought that when we were commissioned and invited to sit on panels and present our unique work and research, plus our findings, to government bodies reporting to and funded by GCHQ, that we would be stood down at the eleventh hour for fear of addressing the issues and uncovering their previous activities and handiwork.

The same issues currently run through the cyber security world as part of its DNA, and that is smoke, mirrors, misdirection and lies. With massive support and evidence, we show why we are in this mess; we can also unequivocally show what part the agencies played and still play to this day, and that is why at every opportunity, we are restricted and 'double hatters' try to undermine our research and findings. In *Stuxnet to Sunburst*, I shared transcripts with the NCSC. It is blatantly clear that although our research and findings evidence the direct correlation and causality between insecure domains and breaches, it is constantly being played down or even dismissed.

The first paragraph of this chapter posed the hypothetical question of what the damage and costs might be if the Internet were to be attacked and offline for a period of time. An article was sent to me by Dr Vladas Leonis earlier today. Dr Leonis agreed yesterday to write the preface for this book, which I am very grateful for and also sure it will be excellent, I am truly very grateful. Dr Leonis (one of the very good guys) was also the first person to read my previous book's early draft, and I would like to publicly extend my eternal thanks for his insight, additions, and concern for its content being made more public than it might already be. When Dr Leonis sent me the article this morning, along with the previous question, I replied in one simple sentence: interesting question; however, if the Internet were down for a day, it would literally also stop all cybercrime…

8

DETERRENCE THEORY AND THE FIVE EYES FAUX PAS

From several tens of $millions 20 years ago lost to digital extortion (cybercrime) to today's $billions spent and $trillions of losses, it is fair to say that no matter who has been at the helm, Bush, Obama, Trump, and now Biden, their leadership in the world of security and infosec has done very little but ultimately had an adverse effect and could be considered as fanning the flames of cybercrime and Ransomware. With the addition and facilitation of crypto currency, criminals can remain pretty anonymous and avoid extortion and money laundering regulations. When you think about it like this, it is a hell of a business model, certainly, for some. As the famous Eagles song goes: 'Did she get tired, or did she just get lazy?' This sums up the main position of the United States, and although cyberattacks and Ransomware are a global phenomenon and problem, the United States suffer some 80% of attacks currently because they are the largest users and have many of the largest and most exploitable targets.

Post the terrorist attacks of 9/11, the US government were herded into signing off $billions to enable global digital dominance, mainly by the United States and to a lesser extent, the United Kingdom. Sure, the Five Eyes were signed up; however, they took more 'cameo' roles. Between the NSA and GCHQ, they identified and seized the opportunity to totally dominate the digital world, to capture all data, harvest it, use it, sell it, and do what they wanted with it, often not bothering to seek any permissions or sanctions. The loss of over 3000 people in the twin towers attack provided them with their motive, along with growing global unrest. They gained more and more funding to develop PRISM and hundreds of other data-capturing and digital intrusion capabilities by developing hundreds of infiltration techniques. The one thing they never stopped to think about or even contemplate, and certainly did not foresee, was what they might do

DOI: 10.1201/9781003278214-8

if, and quite possibly when, their tactics, tools, and methods that they had developed and used globally to exploit weaknesses and vulnerabilities worldwide fell into their (our) adversaries' hands.

The Senators and governments signed Bill after Bill, and $billion after $billion. Bush also signed off on Stuxnet (Olympic Games), and when Obama became President, he continued sanctioning the first digital offensive digital weapon with Biden at his side. The vast sums of money spent by US and UK governments is simply unbelievable, third world debt figures. The creation of thousands and thousands of jobs, many filled by contractors through companies that worked 'favourably' with the governments, witnessed the single biggest increase in labour rates for technical resources, and of course, most companies were owned by ex-colleagues, and with the promise of a Non-Executive Director role or similar upon later retirement, the wheels were suitably oiled and greased. I suspect what started costing $500 ended up costing the US government $2000 and often much more. The 'margin' was used for said greasing.

Roll this out over 20 years and with a ratio of 100 to 1 of people working in cyber offensive versus cyber defensive, it quickly became the default position that Corporate US became overweight, bloated, and simply lazy. More importantly, it also became insecure. Sure, they rode the wave of the digital world, but no one told them, or anyone else for that matter, that they had to take responsibility to make sure it was also secure. Do not forget, the US government were delighted that corporations had little to no idea of how to make sure they were secure, as they could exploit their Insecure positions, and undoubtedly did. Add the fact the numerous Telco companies, social media, and tech giants, in the main, were happy to be 'awarded' major government contracts in return for a backdoor here or there—who would ever know? This position gave the NSA and GCHQ literally access to every IP address, device, and person who ever used any form of technology. They had achieved some amazing capabilities but never thought enough about protecting or securing that position. Even in their own backyard, in the event that enemies could use the same position against them, or us.

I can neither confirm, nor deny if someone somewhere within the governments one day realised the incredible oversight and faux pas they had made. However, when they finally realised, after maybe the first $1 trillion in cybercrime losses, I suspect they pulled out some earlier Deterrence theory papers and declared there was no need to worry, as they could play that hand. They could say that they could do more damage with their cyber firepower; it would work the same as it did with their nuclear program and The Fat Man. Sadly, they were wrong, as we witness every day. As the Senators' committee was told by Paul Nakasone last year, 'Our adversaries are not afraid or scared of us', and this is very much the case. The situation is further compounded by the fact that, over the last twenty years, CEOs, CISOs and Executives simply do not understand what an insecure website means and were rarely, if ever, encouraged to find out. How could one of their own websites that they use to sell items or have a digital presence ever be used against them? Such a suggestion is surely just poppycock. Furthermore, governments are still hiding behind the fact they exploited the digital world and do not want to own up to it. Just look at Crypto AG and OMNISEC, two of the world's largest and most prolific Encryption machine manufacturers who supplied no less than 120 governments. It was only last year that it became known that these Swiss, so-called independent companies were both finally announced as being owned by the CIA, the US government. Both companies manufactured all their Encryption machinery with US government backdoors built in. Even US allies used these machines whilst, unknown to them, the United States were able to simply decrypt their messages and listen in. I cannot comment on the legal position of such clandestine and underhand activities; however, if there were a Cyber Geneva Convention, I am sure this would most certainly not comply.

So back to Deterrence Theory: many experts have applied the theoretical framework of deterrence theory to cyberspace as cyber deterrence. While both typical warfare and cyberwarfare share some characteristics, such as the offensive advantage, given the difficulty and costs of defence, significant differences exist.

The emergence of deterrence theory in the military dates to the 1920s/30s when the first flight bombers were considered unstoppable by defensive measures. Then, strategists thought that large-scale attacks on one's cities could only be prevented if the other side feared (were deterred) counterattacks of similar or even greater magnitude. The first nuclear bombs demonstrated a similar offensive advantage, and Bernard Brodie in 1946, after having witnessed their destructiveness, was among the first to observe that 'from now on the military establishment's chief purpose must be to avert wars'. Deterrence theory gained prominence and developed to its present state during the Cold War nuclear stand-off between the United States and the Soviet Union.

The Second World War was the most expensive war in US history. Adjusted for today's figures, its overall cost was around $4 trillion or, to put it another way, around 75% of the amount that will be lost to cybercrime this year, 2021. With circa 80% of all Cyber losses attributable from the total expected losses globally of $6–7 trillion to the US. So, will Deterrence Theory work in the world of cyberspace? Sadly, I suspect not. The challenge is that, in previous wars, the cost of entry was so high, as opposed to today's cyberattacks, which can be little more than the cost of a keyboard. Even the huge market for Zero Day exploits is inexpensive by comparison.

Deterrence is an old practice which is easily defined and described, even widely deployed but subjectively effective use, however has questionable reliability. Following its prominence post the Second World War, it became the central recourse for international and internal security and stability within states in an era of conflict. Deterrence Theory has been employed to prevent, or at least deter, the destruction of states, societies, and ultimately humanity. Many tout its success, as no nuclear weapons have been used for destructive purposes since 1945. However, Deterrence has been used below that level widely but with varying results. It most certainly is not the Silver Bullet that I suspect the US and UK governments believe it is in today's cyberwar. The cost of entry into the cyberattack world is fractional in comparison, as is the ability to attack from literally anywhere in the world due to the connectivity. Anonymity also is seen as a major benefit, as cyber criminals and nation-states do not wear uniforms and are not easily identifiable. The damage to infrastructure can be in the $billions, including leading to collateral damage, as we witnessed first with Stuxnet over ten years ago.

Furthermore, if the United States have in fact pinned their hopes on Cyber Deterrence, as one could easily guess by their hell-bent focus on Cyber Offensive capabilities over the last two decades, at the cost of nearly all defence, they may be proven to have made a very grave error of judgement, let alone an incredibly costly one. We are witnessing that sheer scale, power, and capability in cyberspace is shifting all theories on previous warfare. The 'underdogs' can actually win due to the inadequate and poor-defensibility position being maintained. David and Goliath is no longer a fairy tale, but reality.

Additionally, deterrence is now much broader and deeper than before. It is under incredible pressure due to technical, cultural, and political viewpoints and operates in a far more intricate and elaborate environment, including Space and Cyberspace. The goal of developing and evidencing empirical theory on deterrence remains on every level incomplete, and whilst deterrence theory remains a fascinating area, it cannot, nor should it, be relied upon.

Being candid for a moment, when people, including security leaders, cannot distinguish between a Secure and Not Secure website and do not understand the dire implications and consequences, it is impossible to see this ending any other way than badly. There are clearly several economies running concurrently: the global economy that we see and that gets reported; The black-market economy that includes drugs, extortion, human trafficking, and cybercrime; and then the grey economy that is run by, well... some from each of these. One can only guess, these are fuelling, and dare I say actively encouraging security incompetence and negligence but encouraging the need and spending. One must question the logic and motive.

In the world of motor racing, where I fortunately enjoyed great success with Aston Martin, we have a saying; 'How do you make a small fortune from motor racing? You start with a large one'. In the cyber world, that large fortune is the global economy and taxpayers. The small fortune is being made by 'favoured and selected' cyber providers and Venture Capitalists. It is a totally unacceptable model and playing into the hands of the few, taking from the masses.

When Critical National Infrastructure organisations such as Energy, Water, and so on are knowingly left in total shambles and with inadequate, lacking, and reckless insecurity and defence with government and regulator knowledge and acceptance, one must ask: is everyone really complacent, or are some being complicit?

As Albert Einstein said; 'If I were silent, I'd be guilty of Complicity'.

9

ENSURING THE SECURITY
OF INSECURITY

In this chapter, we look at the direct correlation between Internet-facing security and breaches. We have researched many hundreds of breached organisations, actually over 1000, often several times a day. The one thing they all have in common across these disparate and often totally unrelated organisations, on different continents and in different time zones, is they all have sub optimal Internet-facing and connected domains. We are not talking a slight variance, either. Our research and findings show a 100% result of hacked organisations typically have security Ratings of F and often a 0. Sometimes it might be an F and 5 or 10. We have never, let me repeat that, we have never found a company with an A+ Rating and 100 score that has been a victim of a breach. One could call it coincidence, or one could call the target group unlucky; however, as mentioned, this is not a high percentage or ratio: it is 100%. Every single organisation from SolarWinds to Donald J. Trump has been maintaining sub optimal domains and, on many occasions, domains with obsolete SSL certificates. As I have mentioned before, this means the certificate has expired, or there is a configuration error rendering the site Not Secure, and being Not Secure, means the authentication and data of the site can lack integrity and data may be being transferred in plaintext form, that is to say, not encrypted. It does not take a rocket scientist, professor, or even a cybercriminal to know that plaintext data is a Ransomware criminal's main goal to exfiltrate. Once exfiltrated, they can then encrypt it, and only they have the decryption tool. I would go as far to say such situations are at the very top of the list for cybercriminals intent on extortion via Ransomware attacks.

Over the last two years, our findings have seen us assisting the FBI when we discovered a Korean DNS in the central voting system, presenting reports to the Senate Intelligence Committee re the SolarWinds

DOI: 10.1201/9781003278214-9

breach following their domain hijacking, and other government and numerous companies to improve their perimeters and overall security posture. It has culminated with MITRE CWE acknowledging and recognising our findings after we discovered they too were using obsolete SSL certs on their homepage and then addressing them. Rather embarrassingly, displaying a Not Secure text in the MITRE CWE address bar. Our discovery and assistance took one of the world's most revered experts in the field of security, backed and supported by the US government, from a Rating of F and 0 to a much more acceptable and secure position. The fact that these leading experts, advising governments and corporate America, had themselves overlooked, ignored, and were maintaining a Not Secure homepage is a sad indictment of the systemic issue and the amount of focus that this critical area has. In case you are not aware, MITRE CWE are supported and backed by the US Department of Homeland Security and acknowledged as thought leaders in global security. We are hopeful their new listing will be created on the back of our work and accredited accordingly with the adoption of our new Internet security gold standard. Sadly, after many exchanges of emails and assistance that we provided, MITRE CWE seem to have taken a vow of silence. They did thank us, though, at the time.

We are fortunate to have Industry experts within and as part of our extended team—collectively much more than 100 years of thought leadership including government experts, professors, PhDs, and long-serving leaders. Our research and findings have been analysed and tested hundreds of times. We no longer hypothesise that there may be a correlation between Internet insecurity and breaches; we make the statement that there is a direct correlation between insecure websites and being targeted and breached. It is no longer a conversation, a debate of egos or subjective opinions: it is simply a fact. As I recently wrote as part of a paper, if the Internet were able to be turned off, no further cyberattacks would be able to take place. Think about that for a minute. The very same connectivity that is enjoyed and facilitates commerce and communication is the very same connectivity that is used to target and launch attacks. This is made possible due to poor security practices at the Internet, which are typically, as was the case at MITRE CWE, overlooked, ignored, or even non-existent.

The question we cannot answer, although we certainly have first-hand experience and our own beliefs, is why governments are so reluctant to adopt and share the intelligence to vastly improve security and to enable the visualisation of what good and bad really does look like? We touched on the NCSC's Web checker in an earlier chapter and then found they, and No. 10 Downing Street, had insecure domains, so either Web checker is not as good as it certainly should be, or needs be, or the NCSC are simply not bothering to 'check their own web' connections. Either way, exposed vulnerabilities cannot be underestimated, understated, or ignored.

We all know the NCSC are the public facing arm of GCHQ and that they have the United Kingdom's, indeed, the world's, security as their core function. It is pleasing, then, to see their Internet-facing domains rated with a respectable B+ and a score of 80/100. The one single thing that would give the NCSC a perfect Rating of A+ and 100 would to be to have a valid CSP (Content Security Policy). However, this Rating and score are certainly representative of a very good and secure position. Quick question here: if this were not an important area, why would the NCSC aspire to ensure their rating was good and they were secure, and why is it taught as part of all Infosec certifications? There is no coincidence. In a later chapter on the Education sector, I will recount the story of the ex-GCHQ senior analyst who confirmed they had been using these techniques as far back as the 1990s to gain access to target companies. In fact, the Belgian telco operator Belgacom sued GCHQ for infiltrating them between 2010 and 2013. If some of the tactics and methods used by our own governments were used by non-government agencies and people, it would certainly be illegal. That activity is now termed as CYBERCRIME...

Whilst briefly touching on Education, the Harris Federation, a group of numerous colleges, were breached on the 23 March 2021 with a Ransomware attack rendering systems locked and data exfiltrated until a ransom payment was made. In a statement the following week, the NCSC stated that the Education sector was witnessing many more such attacks and informed the Department for Education (DfE) and colleges of the danger. Interestingly, the warnings and information came a full six months after we had alerted the Association of Colleges (AOC), Joint Information Systems Committee (JISC), and DfE. A copy of a letter to the UK minister for Education, the Rt Hon Gavin Williamson, was cc'd to the NCSC several weeks before, and no acknowledgment or response was received.

Furthermore, a cursory note was encouraged by the NCSC to be placed in the colleges' handbooks as part of addressing the issue. The Harris Federation, along with most colleges, had security Ratings of F and 0, most still do.

In January 2020, easyJet suffered a breach and called in the NCSC to assist them, along with a major cyber security firm. It was not until several weeks later that easyJet announced the breach in April, at which time we commenced our own investigations and research into their Internet-facing security. What we found, several weeks post breach, was a systemic plethora of insecure domains due to obsolete SSL/TLS digital certificates, misconfigurations, and a raft of CVEs with dozens of easily exploitable positions. It was like a car crash in slow motion, and yet, as our time-stamped screen shots clearly evidenced, easyJet have unbelievably retained their incredibly poor F Rating and a score of 0. Put simply, like the Harris Foundation, their security could not be worse. EasyJet still have a woeful security Rating and Not Secure domains a full year after disclosing their breach. This is in total contradiction and contravention of all privacy laws pertaining to GDPR and UKDPA.

In 2020, Australia were taking a constant hammering, which, according to Scott Morrison, Australia's Prime Minister, heralded from China. He was very vocal in accusing the Chinese predominantly of continuous cyberattacks. Last weekend, the Australian government was literally shut down due to a cyberattack at its very heart which caused major disruption and chaos. We have been in conversations with the Australian government via their DOD (Department of Defence), whom the government initially passed us on to over six months ago. We have provided case after case, and the DOD totally agreed with our research and findings. Their head of cyber finally said, after we alerted the DOD themselves of personally falling foul of Internet insecurity, however, they could only advise, not enforce. The reason Australia is being bombarded and successfully being hit with cyberattacks is, as our screenshots evidence, they dropped their guard, are totally insecure, and maintain security Ratings of F and 0 across many sectors, including the recently breached Service NSW and other Australian government departments. A current DOD employee said to me, 'That he was Disgusted by the total lack of capability and knowledge'. When I told him of a global journalist wanting to run the research and report on the Reserve Bank of Australia, he asked for a copy when it was printed as they simply did not want to listen.

I could literally fill a book full of organisations, CIs, (Critical Infrastructure) governments, and hundreds of other organisations and across all sectors that have been hacked and that have the same or very similar Ratings of F and scores of 0, Today, we research and check many of the most serious and prolific breached organisations and almost last year decided that Three, the MNO, deserved the award for the worst gross negligence. Three have been hacked several times, possibly three. Several letters to their CEO have resulted in no response, and there they sit since their last breach in the autumn of 2019, maintaining a Not Secure domain due to using an obsolete digital certificate. In other words, over 18 months. SolarWinds, by comparison, were not only a late entrant to the awards but have only maintained their F and 0 Rating for 6 months. We find it preposterous, and there are calls to make such inaction a criminal offense. Getting breached due to oversight and negligence is one thing, it is of course certainly not acceptable. One only must see the Class Action Lawsuits starting to pile up to realise there is a moral and legal position for organisations to ensure when handling and supposedly securing personal data, however, it is much worse to ignore the root cause and take no action to remediate the incompetence and gross negligence post being hacked and possibly paying a Ransom.

We constantly look for answers as to why the NCSC and other intelligence communities might want to dismiss the blatant, obvious correlation and negligence of lacking Internet security and breaches. Even when called in to assist companies such as easyJet, BA, Travelex, Harris Foundation, DfE, and hundreds more, the perimeter defences, that is, where the organisation connects to the Internet, are left unchecked and exploitable. If you are taking any advice, pre or post a breach, with such intelligence, I would personally suggest asking your team to ensure security that has a Rating and score like the NCSC as opposed to one of the breached entities with F and 0. Why might the NSA and GCHQ not educate these companies and every other company—what might the motive be, could it really be ignorance?

To conclude, as long as insecure websites rely on invalid SSL/TLS expired certs or have fundamental and easily exploited vulnerabilities and weaknesses, successful cyberattacks will continue to exponentially increase. As the Head of Cyber Intelligence of the Australian DOD said, we cannot enforce; we can only advise. How much advice do companies and boards, pre and post breach require? The advice and evidence they seek and take are entirely up to them, I know there is a much easier, simpler, and more cost-effective method, and, as the saying has gone for decades, prevention is better than cure, it too is tax efficient, costs substantially less, however, any person that might be complicit, will not be lining their pockets.

The only answer we can come up with is the government and their agencies *do not* want companies to have basic security, as it would spoil their tactics and cramp their style. That may have been true one or two decades ago; however, just to remind the world, cybercrime will account for the equivalent of $6 trillion this year, 2021, making it equivalent to the world's third-largest economy behind China and the United States. That fine balance, along with unsustainable losses and attacks, is rapidly altering, and currently, the US and the UK governments have no answer, solution, or even guidance that address or rebalance it. Do not get me wrong, we have offered, time and time again, to assist many governments; we have greatly helped them with intelligence when they knew nothing about numerous insecure positions. As previously mentioned, this is one of the key reasons we believe they do not want to provide security to the masses and have greatly limited the ability of those that challenge the old, broken ways so that they can continue to practice their own methods.

To change the world and to force desperately needed Planet-Scale change, activities must start with Internet security by design. When Microsoft, CISCO, SolarWinds, and other tech giants get Internet security so woefully wrong and can potentially impact billions of people, surely it is time to think differently, cease the ongoing manipulation and abuse, and actively encourage or as mentioned, enforce security connected to the Internet. Last year we presented a program to Google to do just that. Imagine the behavioural change to make sure your organisation was secure, or else you could not get on Google. Imagine the increase in security and the decrease of insecure organisations but, more importantly, the vast reduction of cybercrime against insecure, exposed, vulnerable, and exploitable companies. The Internet is currently like a raging sea, a Venus Flytrap that is waiting to consume any organisation that gains access and is ill prepared and insecure. Sure, it may not be directly the company's fault, it may be their web host, webmaster, development team, or the DNS or CDN providers; however, no matter who it is, if they continually ignore their Internet security, it will be the organisation that is accountable and responsible.

I fear that the governments and agencies delight in the current position, and by ensuring this position is maintained, they can guarantee their security and at the same time, the insecurity of the masses...

10

TRADITIONAL WARFARE, THE FAT MAN, MISTAKES MADE, AND LESSONS STILL BEING LEARNED AND IGNORED

In 1938, German scientists discovered uranium fussion, and in 1939, Albert Einstein wrote a letter to Franklin Roosevelt. That letter became the founding document of the Department of Energy in the United States. In the 1940s, during the Second World War, the US government believed they needed to beat Hitler in building an atomic bomb. The two options available were enriched uranium or plutonium. In 1943, the US government evicted an area that became known as Hanford Ranch in Hanford, Benton County, Washington, and started building a plutonium development facility. From 1943 to 1987, Hanford was responsible for and created two-thirds of the entire US plutonium and built the equivalent of 1800 bombs of the same size used at Nagasaki (Fat Man) on 9 August 1945.

Hanford today, some 80 years later, has 24 million cubic feet of radiation waste underground and 177 storage tanks containing over 50 million gallons of contaminated waste, and it will take another 75 years before it is safe to try to clean the area, which is known as the United States' most toxic area. The cost is estimated to be $660 billion, although Trump was trying to reduce this by calling high level waste low level waste. I suspect he will not personally get too close or too involved! History has clearly demonstrated that major developments within many fields to ensure offensive dominance are maintained. Cyber warfare, I suspect, will be no different; however, the US and UK agencies certainly encouraged mass scotoma (blind spots) was adopted by their governments and by the masses. The one-upmanship of cyber offensive capability would certainly go on, once in the hands of adversaries, to be used en masse for nefarious means on unprecedented

DOI: 10.1201/9781003278214-10

levels. Just as the governments love taxes derived from cigarettes and alcohol in the short term, they know in the long term the costs to healthcare will far outweigh the short-term financial gains.

In the 1960s, GCHQ started work on securing communications (think encryption and decryption) that would become known as PKI (Public Key Infrastructure) and would go on to be further developed by eminent professionals such as Ralph Merkel, who in 1978 developed PKI. PKI would go on to become globally adopted in the 1990s as a secure mechanism to guarantee digital communication and authentication of the user, and the device. PKI used a framework that relied upon digital certificates and encrypted (digital) keys. You will be familiar with mobile phone Apps such as WhatsApp (now Facebook), Signal, and possibly less well-known Apps such as Wire. The aim of all these Apps was to utilise Encryption and Decryption so that communication, just as PKI set out to achieve, was indeed encrypted between users, and only those with the permission of both parties could read each other's messages, documents, and so on. The exact timing of the NSA's and GCHQ's decision to roll PKI out globally and to ensure it had their own 'plants' is unknown; however, it is suspected it was quite possibly instant and part of the overall strategy. What better way to gain intelligence on one's adversaries and allies alike, when they thought everything was encrypted, safe, and secure? As mentioned previously, the US government went so far to gain total and global capability in this area that they secretly bought and owned two of the world's leading Encryption organisations, namely Crypto AG and Omnisec. Both companies were Swiss companies, who during world wars were supposed to be neutral; however, when this information was confirmed in 2020, it certainly was a huge embarrassment to the Swiss government and totally undermined their neutrality.

Throughout the 1990s, dozens, even hundreds of clandestine operations were designed and developed to enable mass surveillance, data harvesting, and data capture. One of the earlier programmes, ThinThread was commenced to capture certain international calls that went either to, or from an international number. Various telecom companies were 'encouraged' to participate in these programmes for favour on government contracts and, of course, in the name of security and democracy. This became the start of mass telephone intelligence gathering. Post 9/11, General Michael Hayden was tasked to head up the NSA and selected a new type of mass surveillance that included all calls, emails, Internet, digital activities, and so on. This required the utilisation of more cooperation from tech giants and the implementation and assistance to plant more backdoors. Such activity often took the form of planting digital certificates, the very same type that, 23 years previously, Ralph Merkel designed to ensure security, where now being used to gather intelligence (spy) effectively on everyone and send the captured data to the Mothership. As the technical capability, and later ease, of planting digital certificates, the practice became more widespread and so much so that after a while, due to lacking PKI controls and management, the Agencies themselves had no idea where and how many they had planted. Many certificate authorities co-operated, and, as the recent SolarWinds breach confirms, as well as Stuxnet, the first digital weapon, confirmed and proved, the use of digital certificates could carry Malware and malicious code that went totally undetected because they looked and acted as internal certificates that were digitally trusted and often not, in fact, virtually never, checked. SolarWinds certificates were a major factor for over 10,000 clients being subsequently breached, and not one of the upgrade certificates carrying the Malware was checked...

In addition to these facts, it is also a concern that not one single person globally actually knows what digital certificates are on a single device, let alone a company or government with a thousand, ten thousand, or one hundred thousand devices. So, the agencies placed more and more backdoors within systems and enterprises than they could simply keep track of or keep up with. That led to many issues, as we have subsequently discovered when we have uncovered government digital certificates within organisations who never knew of their existence. Furthermore, many of these certificates had full capability and what is known as Admin Access: with the right input, these certificates could provide the user C2 (Command and Control). Imagine a situation within an Energy company like Colonial, a nuclear facility or provider and the repercussions could not be worse. Last year, Oldswater Plant lost C2 for a while, when the levels of chemicals was altered and the cybercriminal simply added three 0s to increase the level of Sodium Hydroxide to dangerous, potentially life-threatening, levels. This was achieved by the adversary gaining Remote Access via unpatched Microsoft technology that had known CVEs that were ignored. It was only sheer good fortune that one of the analysts noticed the cursor moving on a screen that was not manned.

General Michael Hayden oversaw and obtained $billions for dozens of programmes. XKeyscore and STELLARWIND which saw DNI (Digital Network Intelligence) globally and included the utilisation of companies such as Crypto AG, as mentioned previously, the Swiss cryptography and Encryption company that supplied services to over 120 countries, all with backdoor capability for the CIA.

In the early 2000s, stolen, compromised digital certificates carrying illegal code were used to carry the infamous Stuxnet virus. The Stuxnet virus initially caused havoc to Iran's efforts to build nuclear power capability and caused a near-worldwide epidemic. It caused physical collateral damage and the loss of lives in Iran. Stuxnet was part of a family which included Duqu, NotPetya, and several other viruses that are still in the wild today. Wannacry, a descendant of Stuxnet, was used to attack the UK's National Health Service and in many other, similar attacks costing hundreds of £millions and potentially more lives. The stakes are incredibly high.

Over the last several decades, we have seen a major shift from traditional armed combat and kinetic warfare to cyberwar and are experiencing massive losses. As I re-edit this, we are in the midst of the world's first fully blown Cyberwar against Ukraine. Perversely, traditional warfare may have directly affected less people; however, more lost their lives directly as a result. Modern cyberwar has much greater costs, with an estimated total of $6 trillion annually by the end of 2021, this figure is 50% more than the entire costs of the Second World War. The main lesson, I guess, is that, as a race, we must acknowledge mistakes and, given the opportunity, adjust and improve upon attitudes and ways to proceed. Sadly, this message is falling on deaf ears currently, as governments still believe they can punch their way out of the mess. A mess that, due to lack of foresight, consideration and negligence, they failed to plan for and ignored.

We are most certainly at a crossroads between security and privacy and have been for some time; sadly, the two are clearly not natural bedfellows. Of course, we want privacy, and we want security; however, they seem to come at a heavy cost. The underlying challenge in today's modern cyber world is the fact that the very aspect that kept us secure by authenticating devices and users, PKI, has been so successfully manipulated and undermined and reverse-engineered, creating back doors, that it has created opportunities and undermines our security and societies and is collapsing our global economy. Our so-called leaders and experts are seemingly not in any way uncomfortable with this situation, as they ignore research, findings, and evidence which are gathered daily.

We witness Executive Orders by Presidents pledging more $billions; however, this money will only grease more wheels, and more companies that are 'favoured' by the government and DOES NOT necessarily provide any reduction in attacks or provide better Internet security. Quite possibly, they only increase the challenges by being Insecure themselves and by doing so, provide a false sense of security.

When quantum computing finally arrives, as it most certainly will within the next decade or so, it will not be the meek that shall inherit the earth, it will be the Nation State, or criminals with quantum computer capability. It seems no government or indeed experts are willing to make a stand now and halt this totally untenable situation we find ourselves in, and put simply, we do not have 8 years, let alone 80 plus, to get this right. The continued procrastination on doing the right thing and holding those responsible to account has and is causing the majority of problems we witness today. That includes the modern phenomenon of Ransomware. Plaintext data is simply and easily removed from insecure domains using methods and tools designed and developed by the NSA and GCHQ and then companies are held to ransom. The company are loath to say they were totally negligent after all the warnings and press coverage, and the Insurers do not hold their clients to account or even bother checking their security. So much so that the vast majority of Insures are guilty of the same insecure position as their clients. The rot runs deep. The agencies do not want to confirm the tools and methods being used by cybercriminals were of their making, as that would confirm these attacks are in fact, nothing more than own goals. However, it sells newspapers and neatly covers backsides to call these attacks sophisticated. To declare Russian or Chinese Nation State attacks and traits and that the NSA or NCSC are working with the company that were the unsuspecting victims of a Nation State's complex and highly targeted attack. What an absolute crock. The victims were targeted and attacked because they were exposed, vulnerable, and easily exploitable. They fitted the MO and could afford and wanted to avoid data leaks or PII data theft, so they paid up. The attacks were in the main opportunistic because they were easy, and it seems that governments and agencies are quite happy with this cycle and unwilling to change anything but add a note or be with change to look.

When I shared our research and findings with the US, UK, and Australian cyber teams, they agreed it was not ideal; they did not want, however, to see our position shared, adopted, or rolled out to provide better, preventative security. In fact, at one UK nuclear power operator where we had provided deep intelligence and highlighted plethora of woeful security positions, including Russian and Chinese presence with potential C2 digital certificates, GCHQ played it down and told the CNI to refrain from any further work with us and to deny any findings. At this stage, it is really important to understand neither our findings nor the implications are subjective; they are fact, and when one CNI has three known RATs (Remote Access Trojans) on its server and Chinese and Russian infiltration on another and is told to stand down, one really must question what the real motives are.

11

SURVIVORSHIP BIAS

Survivorship bias: It is not the certificates and keys you can see; it's the ones that you can't see and do not know about that will cause you challenges.

In 1943, the US Air Force tasked Abraham Wald with a problem. Too many of their planes were being shot down, so they wanted to increase the number of planes that could take attacks and still return safely. Their thoughts turned to adding extra armour to the most vulnerable parts of the planes. Clearly, too much armour would make the planes too heavy to fly properly, so they could not add extra armour over the entire plane. They asked Wald to tell them how much extra armour to add to the parts of the planes that were being hit most often. To help Wald, they had collected statistics on the bullet holes in planes returning from combat. They presented him the statistics of where on the plane the most bullet holes were recorded. After a short while, Wald supplied his findings and recommendations:

> The answer Wald came up with surprised them. He instructed the Air Force to put the extra armour not where the bullet holes were, but where they were not—on the engines! And how did Wald come up with this answer? Simple. He considered the missing bullet holes. The Air Force had presented Wald with statistics on planes that had returned safely from combat. Wald recognized this as biased sample that told a very distorted and totally incomplete story. There were also a lot of planes at the bottom of the ocean, and Wald correctly hypothesised that these planes were full of bullet holes, in the engines.
>
> *Corporate Finance Institute*

The Air Force followed his advice, and the results were excellent. Immediately more planes started returning safely from combat, saving the lives of countless pilots and crew members. Wald had correctly identified this as not so much a math problem but a problem of survivorship bias, and once you understand this concept, you start seeing it everywhere. Survivorship bias tells a lot of distorted and incomplete stories, and looking for the 'missing bullet holes', as Wald did, can save you from making bad decisions based on inaccurate and incomplete information.

Cryptography and cyber security are very similar to the Wald story, as most people focus on the certificates and keys, they think they know they have (known knowns) and even then, in the majority of cases, struggle to manage them; however, it is not just the certificates and keys that you can see and know about that will cause chaos, service outages, and cyberattacks, harming a company. Just as in the story of Abraham Wald and survivorship bias. It's the ones that you do not know about, cannot see, and do not allocate or allow for (unknown unknowns) that will ultimately cause failure.

A fact few know, however, is how many certificates a standard laptop might have, for example. How many digital certificates might be used, or indeed planted or misused on a gold-standard device? We have scanned more laptops with Whitethorn than I care to remember, and the number always surprises everyone. The number of digital certificates on a typical laptop range between 200,000 and 250,000 certificates, with around 20,000–30,000 unique certificates. When we researched and tested a Critical National Infrastructure organisation last year, we discovered a total of 15 million certificates across a controlled group of devices. Revoked, expired, sanctioned, weak, and expired certificates and those with Admin Access from regions and countries that could simply take C2 due to the privileges they held and with excessive validity periods would mean such C2 could be taken over many decades.

On a global cyber security firm's laptop in a controlled environment in Germany, with their country lead and PKI expert, we discovered some 287,000 certificates with the usual array and plethora of issues and several Chinese certificates with 999-year validity with full admin access and control. We urged action after assisting their PKI expert and several partners within the group up off the flaw. They decided to leave it and, as they do not use Whitethorn, one can only guess they are in the same position. ... The same company, the world's reputedly largest Cyber Security firm suffered a rather embarrassing cyberattack in August 2021. No surprise at all.

As in the case of Wald, the CNI company was barely able to look at and manage the certificates they believed they knew they had, let alone the millions they had no idea of. This position was much better understood by the US and UK governments, and they knew without any hesitation that organisations, including governments, would have no idea at all if a few more digital certificates were added with the ability to send data back via the Internet to the Mothership. You can easily see how this method or blueprint of infiltration, certificate insertion and plants, and then exfiltrating data, could and would be used by cyber criminals once they understood and gained the same tools, the same techniques that had designed and developed by our own governments.

There are few trailblazers and even fewer innovators in the world. Most people follow suit, replicate, or simply copy. Cyber criminals rarely, if ever, innovate. They simply emulate and copy what they have learned from others, and sadly, the majority of cyberattacks use the tried and tested methods previously used by our governments and agencies to digitally eavesdrop on the rest of the world. The techniques and methods are identical; the end game plan and goal might be a tad different, I reiterate, might.

Throughout the world, there are millions of small and medium-sized companies, hundreds of thousands of larger companies, hundreds of governments, and thousands of suppliers within the cyber security business. However, they are simply not working congruently together in the best way to combat common cyber threats—but they could be and certainly should be. SMEs (Small and Medium-Sized Enterprises) find it difficult to purchase cyber security due to cost and/or lack of expertise and therefore currently run the gauntlet by playing an incredibly dangerous game of chance. The very same SMEs make up part of the supply chain ecosystem and supply the bigger companies who in turn pay their workers, and both collectively pay taxes that fund the governments, who then are supposed to lead and advise on security issues. Or at least, that is how it should be. However, it is easy to see the flaws, as the current model simply is not working, and governments are uncomfortably caught out in a conflict of interest.

Governments clearly have their own agendas and rarely do much more than appear as experts periodically and provide questionable advice at best. Let us not forget, cyberattacks are based upon their previous activities and methods.

What is happening is the corporate world is being let down by their governments, who are simply failing themselves, as well as the public. Literally, without exception companies are falling short and failing to fully understand how to protect their own businesses and staff and how to survive cyberattacks. This inevitably leads to major cyber losses, and, unless some radical changes are made, cyberattacks will continue to grow both in terms of frequency and magnitude. This will continue shifting and causing a major economic shift. The $trillions gained by cyber criminals will be further used to fund and fuel more crime, drugs, human trafficking, and cybercrime. This is a hell of a slippery slope, and our governments are guilty of greasing it.

The lack of qualified and capable cyber security resources and talent poses additional challenges that exacerbate the problem further. However, one could also argue there will be fewer companies to protect at the rate we are going. It is a sad fact that the lure of potential large gains may convince a young gun who is very tech savvy and opposed to working on the right side of the street to become a grey hacker or even an all-out criminal. This can be further encouraged by the sheer ignorance and dismissal by many of our current leaders and their lack of knowledge. It is invariably and simply an unbelievable battle to try and make companies more secure. A battle that is unquestionably harder than it is to prove their incompetence and negligence or simply to breach the organisation.

Cyber Security professionals and providers are of course trying their best, but we can do more, much more, to bring more unified solutions to the benefit of not just a few, but all. The messages from governments and experts are unquestionably misleading and confusing and not easy to comprehend. This is creating far too many corporate casualties. We will also run into cash challenges. By 2021, it is predicted that cybercrime costs will exceed $6 trillion; that is a 300% increase over 2020. The fact that Internet security should be robust and fit for purpose is neither a subjective nor opinionated statement, so why do so many companies and governments ignore this fact, act negligently, and use the 'sophisticated' attack card as a get-out-of-jail-free position? Why do we not have television advertising our leadership in the Education, Healthcare, and Financial Services (FS) sectors alerting everyone to the Internet's real-life dangers and what can be done to reduce Internet and domain infiltration? Our experience shows, in reality, it is the total opposite. Lloyd's of London, Bank of England, the Financial Conduct Authority (FCA), Healthcare, the Australian DOD, and thousands more all fall well short of good, basic Internet security, many rely upon obsolete SSL certificates, something that is now deemed a cardinal sin since Google made HTTPS compulsory in 2018, supported by NIST and others, so why the failing and negligence?

We believe—in fact, we know—there is a much better way to bring all these numerous components together, to work congruently and maximise efficiency and resources by providing a more centralised cyber security service for the greater good of us all. A single version of the truth if you like. Do we not have a duty to our children, the next generation, to provide a stable, prosperous society? Sustainability is not just about environmental issues, after all. What if we were to harness and maximise the power of real CSaaS (Cyber Security as a Service) and group best-of-breed technologies and capabilities within several providers—global tech security firms under strict supervised contracts or similar? Such a situation would be incredibly cost effective, have huge global economic benefits, and enable scalable solutions for regions, SMEs, and organisations. With the extraordinary buying power that comes with scale, all companies would be able to afford and have proper, fit-for-purpose cyber security. Cyber insurance premiums would be reduced because of unified cyber standards, cyberattacks would be greatly reduced, and the associated economic problems could be averted.

Maybe such a solution is too utopian for some people, but we would take that over dystopia any day. We need radical ideas to stem this tide of global cyber insecurity and need to get rid of biased commercial services that add huge costs but limited, if any real additional security, often adding to overall insecurity. We need a consistent and congruent approach and greater leadership if we are ever to be able to protect the masses, and that must start at the government level. EO's with promises of $billions being spent, lining the pockets of executives and companies such as SolarWinds and other insecure companies and friend and family businesses, add little to improving the security of the Nation—often quite the opposite.

However, we believe it is our duty as experts within our field to drive, educate, and, with encouragement, force the planet-scale change that is so critically required to make the digital world, our world, a much safer place.

12
AIR INDIA RANSOMWARE FAUX PAS

Over the weekend of 22 and 23 May 2021, India's flagship carrier, Air India, announced that it had been targeted and become a subsequent victim of the earlier data breach and hack at aviation information services provider SITA. Its disclosure came five weeks after it was first notified of the situation. This, we believe may or may not be true; however, our research team was straight on the case to research the breach and discover the facts. A new statement from the airline also confirmed that the personal data of around 4.5 million of its customers had been leaked in the March 2021 breach that SITA had previously confirmed. I am unsure if Air India were or were not breached due to the SITA breach and were looking to apportion blame and culpability; however, as the old saying goes, if you are going to throw stones, best not live in a glass house.

This cyberattack and Ransomware breach followed a spate of other similar Ransomware attacks in the Aviation Industry. We had previously researched and covered several previously (see earlier chapter on the Travel Industry), and those breaches included British Airways, easyJet, Star Alliance, and Malaysian Airways. What we discovered, unsurprisingly, was the patterns were nearly identical, and all could be put down to each of the companies' sub optimal controls and management of Internet-facing and connected domains (websites), as we have also shared previously. Unbelievably, many have failed to subsequently address or remediate this, even after being breached, which is simply preposterous and renders them vulnerable to being attacked again and should be considered complicit by their complacency. To put this into context, take BA, easyJet, and many others, for that matter. They have renewed and possibly upgraded many of their devices, servers, laptops, and so on; however, no sooner are they turned on and connected, than they can become compromised due to the insecure overall position and

DOI: 10.1201/9781003278214-12

the maintained Internet security ratings not being improved in any way. When we have written about such situations, we have often used photos of people with their heads buried in the sand or a box of Band-Aid plasters. It is simply nothing short of lunacy to think for one moment that after replacing a few laptops, everything is, or indeed will be OK.

Looking at Air India, the most recent of the Aviation sector breaches, although it has been widely reported over the last few days, no one had identified the real root cause, that is, until we started researching and evidence the facts. Far too many companies, and indeed major players in the world, such as Microsoft (subject of a Not Secure domain this weekend, also due to an SSL certificate expiry) Lloyd's of London, Aon, central banks, and regulators simply DO NOT understand what Internet security actually means or the fact that insecure domains are constantly used to digitally infiltrate and then exfiltrate PII data from organisations, meaning not only have they been breached, they have not complied with all privacy legislation, such as UKDPA and GDPR. In one case, the Global CISO of Lloyd's of London declared; 'We are perfectly secure' whilst waving an SSL Rating of A+. The fact the SSL was correct and valid meant little, in fact absolutely nothing, to the overall insecure position or Rating of the overall website, which was, and still is, F and 0 due to a basic configuration error.

When people look through pinholes or limited apertures to gain visibility, it becomes an egotistic situation to dispel the false positives that such SSL tests alone provide and looking through a restricted lens without seeing the whole picture is not only incredibly dangerous but is also costing $billions in breaches.

The first screenshot we took of Air India from SSL Labs showed they are really doing a good job as far as their SSL certificate is concerned. The validity, protocol, key exchange, and cipher of the SSL test are good. However, it does not confirm security across the entire domain, just the SSL element. It is like a horse wearing very restricted blinkers to run; the horse is visibility impaired on purpose, and in turn, in the case of the Lloyd's CISO, so was he. He based his declaration about Lloyd's of London's security position being fine on the false positive it created, and he acted upon. I have said this before, and no doubt will say it hundreds of times: the evidence we provide is just that, evidence. It is not subjective and does not require a debate; it is a call to action and requires actioning.

The second screenshot we took, also on the morning of 24 May, showed Air India's website, their homepage, as Not Secure in the address bar. When we looked further, it did not even confirm a certificate at all. It did, however, confirm 45 cookies were being used to improve the customer experience. A customer can go onto their Not Secure website and book, pay, and plan flights whilst being totally insecure due to another misconfiguration.

The last screenshot we took was of the overall security Rating of Air India's Internet-facing connected position. The Ratings of F and 0 correctly confirmed that there are indeed serious security issues that need addressing. To confirm, we screenshot and timestamp everything for any legal disputes or when companies take our Actionable Intelligence that we try to assist them with and then totally ignore us. It allows us to demonstrate their positions pre and post being informed. It is also useful should any Class Action Lawsuits take place later to evidence their position at the time of the breach. When we looked even further at Air India's position, we discovered that a new RSA 2048-bit Digicert certificate was placed on the domain on 9 April 2021 at 01:00 CET which was valid until 11 May 2022 at 00:59 CET. It was at this point we discovered the real error, a totally human error of their server setup and configuration. We cannot retrospectively confirm how long this insecure position had been set; however, we can hypothesise that with the Google change of HTTP to HTTPS in 2018, the problem may have been as old as 3 years. No one noticed or bothered to check, not even when renewing certificates for their homepage, which is nothing short of gross incompetence and negligence when it comes to security.

Whomever at Air India is responsible for their Internet Security and/or PKI had misconfigured the server. The server rightly supports HTTPS; however, is configured to redirect to HTTP, a complete error or was it complicit? In car terms, this is as if a modern car with excellent tyre technology had been fitted with cross-ply tyres from 1950. If you Google HTTPS, you will see this became the standard back in 2018, and any domain/server using the insecure HTTP would be displayed as Not Secure. It may also show the following warning: 'Your connection to this site is not secure. You should not enter any sensitive information on this site (for example, passwords or credit cards) because it could be stolen by attackers' ...

As mentioned, at this point, we cannot confirm how long Air India have maintained their Insecure position or when the error was made; it may date back to 2018. However, what we can confirm is this, let us call it an oversight (lawyers would call it gross negligence), has made them a prime target. By being Not Secure, the domain lacks authentication, and the data can lack integrity and be altered and also can be exfiltrated, manipulated, and abused; furthermore, it could also be captured as plain text, the staple diet of all cyber criminals and Ransomware attackers. Cyber criminals are in many ways just like regular people inasmuch that they want an easy life. To date, of all the hundreds and hundreds of breached organisations we have researched, not one, not a single company, has had an A Rating of their security facing and connected to the Internet. Every single one, without exception, has had a Rating of F and just a handful a D. Cyber criminals use OSINT as part of their reconnaissance to identify exposed, vulnerable, and exploitable companies, and from experience, they find such positions at the majority of companies due to inaccurate or non-existent security postures. This must change for cyberattacks to reduce.

The faux pas, if you will, is their domains, which can be easily and frequently unknowingly infiltrated by using numerous methods and the exfiltration of plain text data, again easily. The plain text data is then encrypted and ransom demanded before the attackers (hopefully) hand over the decryption keys. There are no guarantees here, of course, as we are talking criminals. Organised criminals are far better organised than most teams and individuals tasked with providing security and only need to find a single exploitable insecure position.

Ransomware attacks are, in the main, not sophisticated, or unique. Since the autumn of last year, Ransomware groups have been set up to maximise and share targets and Ransomware negotiation capabilities for a percentage of the actual ransom. It has become a standard model that is being utilised. The saddest part is that our own agencies designed and developed these methods over the last two decades as part of their own mass data collection and harvesting, and they are now being used against every company globally who, through oversight, complacency, and even negligence, allows their domains to become insecure.

Over this weekend, we witnessed Microsoft have one of their domains become Not Secure when their exchange server allowed its digital certificate to expire. This caused many servers to alert those trying to log in with the Not Secure text in the address bar and the warning 'Attackers might be trying to steal your data', in what can only be seen as a major error and blight on Microsoft's control and management of their own PKI and any consequential outages and infiltration. It is too early to say if any nefarious activities took place during the outage; however, Microsoft are under constant attack 24 × 7. If, as I suspect, cyber criminals discovered the digital doors were unmanned and insecure, they would certainly capitalise upon such an insecure position.

Lacking basic security controls and management is costing companies tens, sometimes hundreds of $millions and, collectively across various sectors, $billions. Such attacks are in the main avoidable, however require discipline and constant management, and are the reason we designed and developed Whitehorn Shield. Companies can opt out of being on a Ransomware target list and ensure Internet-facing and connected security is robust and fit for purpose. Governments, Insurers, Leaders, and experts need to drive a planet-scale change, so why are they not? Why is it we gain attention from double hatters trying to dissuade and ridicule the facts as evidenced; why are Ministers burying their heads, and why do Captains of Industry like Lloyd's of London, AON, Zurich, Bank of England, the FCA, the US Treasury, the FBI, NCSC, and GCHQ want our messages and evidence to be swept under the carpet? Why are they not driving global awareness and ensuring they, along with governments and global leading companies like Microsoft and SolarWinds, do not act negligently, leading to breaches and infiltration? It makes no sense no matter which way you think they want to play it. We remain of the opinion and are convinced that the NSA and GCHQ are blinding the masses with science and are happy with the security of insecurity that they control; however, if they are relying upon their offensive capability to dissuade our adversaries from attacking, surely, they are acting foolishly, and placing the world's economic future in the balance and at risk...

13

MOST COMMON WEBSITE VULNERABILITIES AND ATTACKS

With the massive uptake of digital marketing and explosion of websites over the last decade or so, it is fair to say some, far too many in fact, fall through the security gaps and become insecure. That is not an excuse; it is sadly a fact. Take NASA, for example. The last time we looked, they had over 20,000 domains—yes, that is not a typo: over 20,000. Less than 5% are active, the rest are legacy, and many have security issues. Furthermore, when we tracked the upward curve in website numbers and laid over the data for increased cybercrime costs, the curve was virtually identical. It should come as no surprise, then, that websites are among the very first place cyber criminals look to gain access for their illegal and nefarious cybercrime activities. This should no longer come as a surprise.

We covered the difference between SSL test ratings and full domain security ratings; however, we thought in this chapter, we would list some of the most common issues that, when not managed well, lead to exploitable vulnerabilities. Some are more serious than others; however, this list is a strong starting point. Knowing that cyber criminals are always looking for easy, insecure targets would suggest that if the basics are done, and done well, a company that demonstrates good basic security will certainly not be the first in line to fall victim to a breach. As previously mentioned, we have yet to research a breached company with an A-rated website. This is not a coincidence.

Let us try to keep this as straightforward as possible and not too technical. I will leave that to others; however, the following list covers many of the most widely used attack methods and makes up some of the metrics that we scan for to provide an overall security rating.

DOI: 10.1201/9781003278214-13

Cross-Site Scripting

XSS (Cross-Site Scripting) attacks are one of the most, if not the most, common attacks, accounting for around 40% of all attacks. XSS attacks are not overly sophisticated however frequently used by many cyber attackers, typically using scripts that others have developed and that are readily available on the Dark Web Cross-Site Scripting targets users of websites instead of the website application itself. Code is inserted into vulnerable (insecure) websites and then executed by the unsuspecting visitors. The code can compromise the users' accounts, activate Trojans, or modify the website's content to trick users into providing additional information and PII data. The best way to defend against XSS is use a WAF (Web Application Firewall). A WAF acts as a filter that can identify and block malicious requests to a website. X-XSS has become the No. 3 most used exploit in the OWASP Top Ten.

Injection Attacks

Another high-risk factor for websites is SQL injection, listed by the OWASP (Open Web Application Security Project) as a major, top ten attack threat. This injection attack method directly targets and attacks the website and the server's database. The attacker inserts a piece of code which can discover and uncover data and user inputs. It enables modification and can compromise the application. Protecting a website against such attacks typically comes down to how well the code has been written and how well it is secured. A workflow authentication is also a worthwhile option.

Man-in-the-Middle Attacks

MiTM attacks are frequently used when websites have not encrypted their data and the data is in plain text. This is very commonly used for Ransomware attacks, enabling plain text to be exfiltrated, encrypted, and then sold back to the victim along with decryption keys. Attackers target vulnerable websites looking for easily available PII data, either data at rest or in transit. When the data is not encrypted, it can be read as easily as the text in this sentence and usually breaches all privacy regulations, especially if it captures PII data. One of the best ways to protect against and mitigate MiTM attacks is to ensure valid SSL/TLS certificates are on the website. This sounds easy; however, as this book and the previous book testify and evidence, many times over, companies, including giants like Microsoft, often get this wrong and typically suffer dire consequences as a result.

Distributed Denial of Service

DDoS (Distributed Denial of Service) attacks are typically attacks that render a website unavailable and offline temporarily, sometimes permanently. By overwhelming the website's servers with requests, and therefore the site is unavailable for legitimate users, hence the term denial of service. Botnets are usually used to bombard the servers with requests utilising infected computers. It is also quite common for DDoS attacks to distract security systems whilst exploiting other vulnerabilities. One of the most popular methods to mitigate a DDoS attack is to use a CDN; a load balancer and scalable resources are also worthy additions. A WAF should also be utilised to prevent a DDoS masking other attacks such as the injection of XSS.

Brute Force Attacks

One of the worst vulnerabilities we witness is when we uncover Not Secure login domains that are using obsolete SSL/TLS which renders the website wide open to abuse. A Brute Force Attack is a straightforward method for accessing login credentials to gain access, typically gain certain privileges, and ultimately gain Digital Trust. If an assailant is using social engineering, it is usually quite easy to guess passwords and gain access, which can then be used for further infiltration. The best way of protecting login information is to ensure the website is using a valid SSL/TLS certificate and also by using 2FA (Two-Factor Authentication). Site owners have responsibilities to control this and their users.

Phishing

Phishing attacks are not directly aimed at websites necessarily but utilise email addresses. Phishing is listed by the FBI as the most-used form of Social Engineering cybercrime. Phishing campaigns (Spear Phishing) can certainly compromise system integrity. The attack uses misdirection as assailants look to gain email access and take over an email account pretending to be someone they are not. By way of an example, the FBI in the fall of 2021 suffered a cyberattack. Due to an Insecure subdomain and server, the server, more than likely an MX was taken over. One hundred thousand FBI emails were sent out to unsuspecting recipients. The FBI themselves did not send the emails, however, FBI servers were used to send legitimate FBI emails as if they had. Phishing attacks can be used as part of a larger attack and use deception to encourage sharing information or to make payments urgently to avoid further issues. Avoidance of Phishing attacks can be down to internal organisations' training and diligence, however, insecure Domain Name Systems can be used to gain backdoor access and take over servers as was, we believe, the case above. There are several Phishing solutions on the market; some work well, some not so much. In this area, being vigilant is the very best method, and urgent requests for immediate payments from superiors are best checked thoroughly before being made. They have, however, caught many major organisations out, paying $millions to new customers/clients.

Third-Party Code

Most websites utilise content from third parties. It is the website owner's responsibility to ensure all third-party code used to make up their all singing, all dancing website is in fact secure. By way of example, last year The Canadian government suffered a hack which included their Tax Offices. We were asked to help via one of our colleagues in the region who had a relationship with some of the senior government officials. When we started researching, it was not too long before we discovered that the flag that was being used by all this government's websites was written in code that put the government websites in a highly vulnerable position; no one had checked that, and insecure government websites had been published and were being maintained as Not Secure. Unfortunately, the Canadian government had already been breached and, in typical fashion, only bothered to check after the event. The root cause of the breach was down to third-party code that caused the entire domain to be exposed, vulnerable, and exploitable.

To mitigate the risk of third-party code making websites insecure, website owners/developers and Infosec leads must ensure all plugins are up to date and plugins such as WordPress (a well-known weakness and vulnerability) as well as others are also up to date.

Zero Day Attacks

ZDAs (Zero Day Attacks) are used mainly by well-funded or financed Nation State cyber groups. They take their name from the fact they are a new, unknown attack vector and capability, and therefore there are Zero Days (ZD or 0 days) of experience to combat the attack. It is effectively a new software vulnerability that has not yet been encountered or remediated. Attackers can gain information and intelligence and discover loopholes before updates are made public to address them. Often patches and updates are months behind the curve of a ZD, and as such, the ZD can be exploited for some period before anyone is the wiser. ZDs, once known about, are the catalyst for the updates and patches. There is a very buoyant Black Market for cyber criminals and governments to stockpile Zero Day Exploits (which can cost six or even seven figures) to gain a digital advantage. It is virtually impossible to be proactive and prevent ZDAs, apart from good cyber hygiene; however, it is critical to address, update, and upgrade software as soon as it is made available.

Cookies

Cookies in the first instance can be harmless and were originally used to ensure the user experience was smooth and did not require repetitive logins and data repetition. However, cyber criminals can also use cookies for many nefarious activities such as making a website appear to be unavailable to users, or insert a cookie for data capture. When returning to a website, users are sent a cookie back to the web browser. A cybercriminal can alter that cookie in many ways and plant cookies as they wish, especially if there is a security issue. If the number of cookies is exceeded, a website can become unavailable until the cookies are deleted. The law on the use of cookies is constantly a bone of contention, and cookies are used by companies to track web browsing history and activity. It is always best to opt out of cookies when given the option. It is possible, although a pain for those just wanting a website service, to see exactly what the cookies are used for, and there are, as I mention, calls to limit the tracking and activity of users as part of a wider privacy drive. On some sites, it has become annoyingly complex to opt out of cookies and to trawl through that option as opposed to 'Accept All'. This is nothing more than a marketing ploy and should, wherever possible, be avoided. All websites want footfall and business conversion in whatever form of metrics that are used. Legislation is slow to respond; however, by boycotting websites because of the intrusion, it will drive behavioural changes.

More recently CSP has been added to bolster website security. A CSP is a HTTP header that enables operators to have more control over where resources on their site can be loaded from. The use of a CSP is the best way to prevent XSS (see previously). It is acknowledged that it is not as easy to retro fit a CSP; however, CSP has become mandatory for all new websites and highly recommended for all high-profile and high-traffic websites. The other major benefit of using a CSP is it disables the use of unsafe JavaScript and inline JavaScript, meaning improperly escaped user inputs can generate code that is interpreted as JavaScript. Using a CSP is the single most effective method to eliminate XSS attacks against a site.

We know that websites can also be used for Watering Hole and Drive By attacks as well as domain hijacking and takeover (SolarWinds). We also appreciate that it is a full-time task to ensure that websites are secure. The changes to security for websites come thick and fast but nowhere near as fast as attacks. With an estimated 200,000 website attacks a day, it has never been more important, or critical to have proper controls and management in place. Companies' domains can certainly be key to their online presence and success; they can also be used as part of an overall attack and infiltration strategy. $billion companies such as SolarWinds can and do fall victim to attacks that commence as an attack on an insecure domain that are using obsolete SSL's and then become a domain hijacking due to being insecure, unmanaged, and uncontrolled. In the case of SolarWinds, that attack led to Domain Admin Access (the keys to the kingdom), and tens of thousands of companies never once stopped to ask if the SolarWinds digital certificate updates were trustworthy; they simply downloaded them, totally unaware of the malicious Sunburst code that had been planted within their code. We would also suggest no due diligence was requested or insisted upon even by government departments.

The Internet is indeed an incredible tool for marketing, sales, product launches, communication and much more; however, it can and will bite hard and often does if left to its own, insecure devices. It will put companies out of business and, as mentioned previously, is creating the word's single largest shift in economic terms, with over $6 trillion in 2021 being the cost and losses to cybercrime annually, predicted to top $10 trillion by 2025.

Many have said (including Ginni Rometty, the former CEO of IBM) that cyberattacks are the single largest threat to Companies and our economic future, and yet why are so many great, experienced experts twiddling their thumbs and so many Captains of Industry, as we have mentioned, happily ignoring evidence and the facts? As one senior MOD official said to me, the costs in terms of $ and lives is simply not large enough yet to get the attention that it urgently requires.

Maybe we need a central bank or financial regulator to be the victim of a hack. From our research, that will not be too far away…

14

THE OLD LADY OF THREADNEEDLE STREET AND THE FCA

The 'Old Lady' of Threadneedle Street, the Bank of England, has been headquartered in the centre of the City of London since 1797. As a regulator and central bank, the Bank of England does not offer consumer banking services, nor has it for many years. It does, however, still manage some public-facing services, such as exchanging superseded bank notes. It also ceased providing personal banking services to its staff in 2016.

The Bank of England is the United Kingdom's central bank and created the model most banks around the world are based upon. First established in 1694 to act as the bank for the UK's government, which it still is today, the Bank of England is the world's eighth-oldest bank. The Bank of England was nationalised in 1946, the year after the Second World War, after being privately owned by stockholders since its foundation. To date, the bank, although nationalised, has 3% ownership by private shareholders whose identity remains a secret; apparently the bank is not at liberty to divulge who they are. The Bank of England confirmed that interest is paid out twice a year to these anonymous shareholders.

In 1998, the Bank of England became an independent public organisation, wholly owned by the Treasury Solicitor on behalf of the government and with the independence to set monetary policy. The Bank of England is one of only eight banks authorised to issue banknotes, has exclusive rights to do so in England and Wales, and regulates the issue of banknotes in Scotland and Ireland. The bank's Monetary Policy Committee has a devolved responsibility for managing monetary policy. The Treasury has reserve powers to order the committee 'if required in the interest of the public and in extreme

DOI: 10.1201/9781003278214-14

economic circumstances'. Such an order must have Parliament backing and support within 28 days. The bank held its first Financial Policy Committee in June 2011 as a macroprudential regulator to oversee regulation of the United Kingdom's financial sector.

The Governor of the Bank of England, Andrew Bailey, was, until being recently appointed to his current role on 16 March 2020, the Chief Executive at the FCA (Financial Conduct Authority), previously known as the Financial Services Authority. Before this role, Mr Bailey had served as the Deputy Governor of the Bank of England, a long way from his earlier days at the bank as a Chief Cashier from January 2004 to April 2011.

During the financial crisis in late 2007 to 2011, Mr Bailey was responsible for the bank's special operations to resolve the challenges within the banking sector. On 1 April 2013, Mr Bailey became the Chief Executive of the Prudential Regulation Authority, becoming the first Deputy Governor of the Bank of England for Prudential Regulation.

It is more confusing than it might need to be however, think of the Bank of England, the Prudential Regulator, and the Financial Conduct Authority as working congruently across all sectors of Financial Services, which includes Insurance. It would not be unreasonable to think of this group as being incredibly influential in the world of regulation and banking not only in the United Kingdom but globally.

On 24 April 2020, we reached out to several of our contacts at the Bank of England, as our research had alerted us that the bank had 'overlooked' a digital certificate renewal on their homepage. This, as we know, is a huge, and somewhat embarrassing error and creates all manner of security issues, including making the bank exposed, vulnerable, and exploitable to cyberattacks. We swapped emails with several of our senior contacts at the bank and included a timestamped screenshot of SSL Labs showing no certificate. The intelligence was neither subjective or opinionated; it was fact and, in simple terms of Internet connectivity and security, as bad as it could be. We also shared the same information with Dr Ian Levy of the NCSC confirming the intelligence was in fact our own Central Bank and received no reply.

A week passed and I sent a follow-up mail to my primary contact, who then confirmed they were off sick recovering from health issues. Of course, I was as sympathetic as I could be however, the fact of the matter was the Central Bank was exposed to an attack. I urged the details be shared with the appropriate person within the bank. At this point, I could not avoid thinking of the repercussions should cyber criminals gain access through such security negligence and what damage and demands they could impose. The US Treasury had been infiltrated recently through the SolarWinds debacle, so literally nowhere was safe, and that was even more the case when the digital front doors were left wide open and unmanned.

I was finally given the name of a person at the bank to look up on LinkedIn. I was not given an email or introduction, just a name for me to run around trying to alert our own central bank of their error. I sent a mail via LinkedIn and two days later received a reply. I sent a set of screenshots showing the missing SSL and a screenshot of the mismatched certificate and Not Secure screenshot. The message received on 7 May said:

> Morning Andy. Thank you for getting in touch. The Bank has a formal Vulnerability Disclosure policy and process which you can find at our website. For your awareness, no services sit behind the homepage, the Bank's website is under the www.alias. However, we can appreciate that it is poor user experience and something we are seeking to rectify promptly with a 301-permanent redirect. If you feel that you have further information on this, then we would welcome you providing this via the link above. Regards.

I did indeed have much more to share and actionable intelligence but was by now pretty peeved at running around, sending emails, and explaining their insecure issues and sent an email reply confirming the information we had shared was in good faith and that as an organisation we would gladly engage; we were not in a position to sit completing Vulnerability Disclosures for organisations of the FBI, MITRE CWE, and the NCSC or the Bank of England as we had previously done on numerous occasions and receive barely any gratitude or recognition. We are all for helping people; however, all of those we were helping were indeed being paid to do their jobs and were not doing them very well, in fact, some might say appallingly. I wonder how many took accolades from the information we shared and how much we had saved them by averting infiltration and even potential breaches. The email exchanges with the Bank of England stopped from there, and on 17 May, our research showed that the Bank of England had now corrected the error we had pointed out and alerted them to. No confirmation, no gratitude from any quarter, just a sneaky remediation and hopefully no one will notice. We use the screenshot that is timestamped as evidence of the major error made. Furthermore, as my last email confirmed, there were other similar issues that remained unaddressed which are creating other, major vulnerabilities in a near-identical fashion to Lloyd's of London, which I have informed several times. To put this into perspective, when we first alerted the Bank of England of their issues, their overall security Rating was at F and 0. After they addressed the SSL, we alerted them to, it only became a D and 35/100, hardly what you would say is first rate for a central bank which lacks an HTTP Strict Transport Security (HSTS) header and redirects correctly to HTTPS but to another HTTP first and is open to Cross-Site Scripting and MiTM attacks. No matter what data is or is not being kept or sits behind the bankofengland.co.uk website, such an oversight is nothing short of security incompetence and negligence.

The research on the Bank of England was part of a larger research paper and exercise across the Financial Services, central banks, and regulators. As part of this research, the Financial Conduct Authority were also included.

The FCA is a financial regulatory body that operates independently of the UK government and is financed by charging fees to members of the Financial Services Industry. The FCA regulates financial firms providing services to consumers and is responsible for maintaining the integrity of the UK's financial market. The FCA was formed on 1 April 2013 after being the FSA previously. The FCA, Prudential Regulator, and Bank of England are intrinsically linked and work closely together to ensure monetary policies, financial stability, and regulations are upheld. Without either party, the Financial Services market could simply collapse and go into freefall.

On 15 April, I reached out to a senior Risk and Technical Specialist at the FCA who kindly responded. I shared our concern and the fact that the FCA had a security rating connected to the Internet of F and 10/100 and was concerned that if cyber criminals discovered the insecure positions, they could launch a successful and quite likely unknown attack on the regulator. I was provided with her FCA email and then emailed screenshots and further information. I was thanked and told they would discuss internally. I was also given the number and email for their whistle@fca.org.uk website. I was further introduced to the FCA CISO, who sent me an email on 24 April copying their threat intelligence team and requesting I send them further information. I had previously sent an introduction overview and request on LinkedIn to their CISO on 19 April 2019 which went unanswered. I sent an email reply and confirmed my concern; I sent a copy of the date-stamped evidence and screenshot. Given the working relationship between the FCA and the Bank of England, I also raised the concerns from our research and was told they are a separate entity and that I should try contacting them, which is exactly what we did, as noted above.

I sent another email on 26 April asking when I should expect to hear from the CSO office, as I had not, and the security Rating was unchanged at F and 10/100. I received an email reply from the FCA CISO as follows:

> Andrew, as per my email on Friday, if you would like to report technical details of an issue you have uncovered to my counter threat unit, please do so. We will of course investigate any valid concern raised by external partners, in addition to the internal assurance activities we routinely undertake. With regards to the Bank of England, they are an independent organisation, and you will need to contact them directly. If this is a sales call, then I would request you be clear and transparent upon the basis of this conversation.

Let us recap for a moment. We undertook research, at our cost and time. We sent several emails informing and alerting the Bank of England and the FCA of their insecure positions that our research has discovered and copied in the NCSC. These positions showed each organisation had Ratings of F and 0 and F and 10/100. Further research confirmed redirection issues; third-party content in HTTP, making the domain exploitable; and Cross-Site Scripting and MiTM issues, to name a few. Not once had we mentioned anything about sales or held back intelligence on these findings, and on both occasions, we met with a degree of resistance and lack of appreciation, and yet still both organisations remain insecure, meaning a lack of action on their behalf. The Bank of England still have subdomains using obsolete SSL certificates, and the FCA still have a woeful security Rating of F and 10/100. The Bank of England is slightly better, with a D and 35/100. In both cases, I am confident to say suffering a successful cyberattack would see them rushing around like rabbits in headlights, and yet our research has been shared, clearly showing a lack of knowledge and capability and negligence of their Internet-connected security position. The Bank of England finally addressed the single SSL issue we alerted them to after two weeks, and the FCA have not requested to engage professionally, and both remain insecure. Please, let us not forget, we are talking about THE UK Central Bank and THE UK Financial Regulator here, not a small insurance broker or water treatment plant. This situation, one we have shared several times and notified the CEO and CISO of on several occasions, is being ignored, and both organisations remain exposed, vulnerable, and exploitable. I suspect any Ransomware or Nation State–backed group would very much like to add either or both to their list of victims.

The position of the executives and those responsible for security must be questioned and challenged. A successful attack on either organisation could have potentially catastrophic repercussions and implications, not just across the UK Financial Sector but globally.

15

MITRE CWE AND RANSOM TASK FORCE

Internet security is not easy. We know and acknowledge that; however, we need to ensure websites are secure, as cybercriminals only need a single access point or a single vulnerability to exploit, and they know where to look and how to find them. More importantly, they also know how to exploit them. One of the cardinal sins in my opinion is a domain (a homepage) that is Not Secure due to security negligence, it is simply unforgivable and relying on an obsolete or invalid SSL. It may be mismatched, which is not unusual: by being issued to a different name, the domain www.example.com could be www.example1.com, meaning the domain would be Not Secure due to the mismatched cert. It could be expired if it were issued one year and 5 days ago and valid for a year but ran out 5 days ago, this would also make the domain Not Secure. We have witnessed SSL certificates stay expired for years and not be picked up. One such company who made Atomic Bombs for the DOD and DHS in the United States maintained a Not Secure domain for several years until they finally listened to us after several emails.

It is blatantly clear that not only companies, but also far too many security professionals simply do not understand what an insecure domain means, but also casual visitors and users do not realise the critical importance of ensuring they are on secure domains. When the Not Secure text is in the address bar instead of a padlock, which has been in place since Google and others enforced it in 2018, it means a domain that displays Not Secure. There is no trickery, it is in fact exactly that, NOT SECURE; it warns cyber attackers might be trying to steal PII data, credit card details, and so on. Yet day after day, literally millions of insecure websites are visited and PII data is captured for nefarious purposes, more times than not without any knowledge of what has happened. Think of it as Digital Identity Theft. It can of

DOI: 10.1201/9781003278214-15

course get much worse, such as when SolarWinds lost command and control due to a domain being hijacked and taken over. We often hear of people saying their Not Secure website doesn't store data or capture information. It may have 40 cookies, however, and capture your unique IP and other details. It is NEVER OK for a live website to maintain a mismatched, misconfigured, or expired SSL. It shows and indeed confirms carelessness and lack of security control and management. Such websites are the staple diet and targets of cybercriminals, who happily attack 200,000 websites a day.

You will have heard the question I am sure, 'Who polices the police?' and understand its meaning. In the world of security, egos can typically be rather large, and as such, when security experts are found to have overlooked or ignored basic security connected to the Internet, it is usually at that point the old 'there is nothing on it, nothing to see we know and are moving domains' and so on is heard. You will never hear a security expert, certainly not publicly, say, 'Oh bummer, we forgot that; it is my fault that we have been infiltrated due to my incompetence and neglect of our Internet security'. So, it came as something of a shock when we started researching a number of cyber security organisations to find they were themselves guilty of being insecure, some with the cardinal sin of having homepages displaying the Not Secure text in the address bar. The two following examples show why discipline is unbelievably lacking in major security organisations and, in these two examples, backed by the US government.

MITRE CWE is a community-developed list of software and hardware weakness types. It serves as a common language, a measuring stick for security tools, and a baseline for weakness identification, migration, and prevention efforts. MITRE CWE list the most prolific and dangerous vulnerabilities and weaknesses and are the go-to guys for all things security. MITRE CWE are supported by the DHS (Department of Homeland Security) and CISA and managed by the HSSEDI (Homeland Security Systems Engineering and Development Institute). MITRE CWE are unequivocally globally recognised as thought leaders in the security sector.

Imagine our surprise when on 11 March 2020 we discovered and wrote to MITRE CWE to confirm that they were maintaining a visibly Not Secure homepage. This situation had serious repercussions for the domain, its content, and its connections both up- and downstream, let alone a rather embarrassing and ironic situation. Furthermore, back to my earlier comment, 'Who is policing the police?' A copy of my first letter follows:

Dear MITRE CWE Community.

We have been working across numerous sectors and will be utilising various MITRE CWE's that the community list for digital certificates such as the following:

CWE 287 Improper Authentication
CWE 296 Improper Certificate's Chain of Trust
CWE 298 Improper Validation of Certificate Expiration
CWE 599 Missing Validation of Certificate
CWE 322 Key Exchange without Entity Authentication

Furthermore, in the last week, Microsoft have issued CVE2021–26855 that uses insecure Port 443 to launch attacks and when it finds such an instance, due to an obsolete or misconfigured TLS/SSL certificates, enables the launch of Server-Side Forgery (SRRF) attacks sending arbitrary HTTP requests and authentication to the server. If HTTPS were being used, such attacks would not be successful.

Given our findings and experience, from the White House to the US Treasury, from SolarWinds to the Vatican, all have been found to be falling foul of the lack of control and management of Internet security and PKI. We believe a substantial number of organisations are initially targeted by virtue of technology readily available to identify Not Secure domains and then to launch easy attacks due to the organisation's insecure position. Often such attacks are not even known about until the breach manifests itself.

We developed an AI technology and business model to provide daily assurance and monthly reporting which can also support audits, cyber insurance score carding for both initial policies and potentially claims and also for good basic cyber hygiene. With 200k attacks per day and cyber criminals launching attacks from thousands of miles away, their targets are vulnerable and with weak Internet connections. Unfortunately, as we read all the time, offensive capability is right up there, defensive is sadly not.

Finally, as cyber experts, we all know that domain hijacking, as happened to SolarWinds is made all the easier when organisations do not have control or management of what may be a disparate set of domains and subdomains, even launching new sites often go published with misconfigured or mismatched certificates which renders the domain as Not Secure. Such a position can enable domain hijacking as mentioned, domain takeover (www. avsvmcloud(.)com) Man in the Middle Attacks, DDOS, lack of domain authentication, data being maintained in plaintext (major factor for Ransomware increase) and ultimately, C2 (command and control). Domain Admin Access is a real live threat enabling an adversary to gain privileges and full access as we have recently witnessed.

There is a reason cybercrime has created the world's third largest economy by virtue of revenues, and that growth can be directly attributed to insecure Internet access, lax basic security, and lack of adoption of HTTPS from HTTP since 2018. The likelihood of continued attacks and this being a CWE are extremely high, in fact, it can be considered as a certainty.

Finally, and rather embarrassingly, cwe.mitre.org itself is falling foul of all the above CWE's by virtue of not having a valid TLS cert in place currently which confirms the entire contents of my mail. Privacy laws such as UKDPA, DPA, GDPR and similar are not being met and immaterial of what data is, or is not being maintained, the fact an IP address is captured on a Not Secure domain constitutes PII data.

I look forward to hearing from you in due course.

I received a polite note sometime later suggesting we were not right, as an SSL Qualys scan showed they were OK (the same comment made by the ill-informed CISO at Lloyd's) and fast becoming a false positive that Industry leaders are incorrectly judging their security on. We replied and after swapping emails and pointing out the Apache web server was issuing root certificates and the certificate chain was misconfigured. Remember the CISO at Lloyd's debated strongly that their Internet Rating of F and 0 was incorrect because he had scanned using SSL Labs, which showed a solid A Rating, as indeed it would, as it was checking only the SSL certificate, not everything else.

To cut a long story short, after MITRE CWE addressed the security errors we had alerted them too and they were blissfully unaware of, yet totally exposed because of, we asked MITRE CWE to allocate a new CWE to provide information about this common vulnerability and threat; however, once we had assisted them, they seemed to fall off the earth's surface, and we have never heard from them since, which, after saving their backside, seems a tad rude and unreasonable. Maybe they had something to hide? We thought it was a breakthrough to be acknowledged as thought leaders in the field; however, all MITRE CWE wanted to do was get rid of us, and never to be mentioned again. I have sent several emails subsequently without response.

The second organisation to literally shock, and also bitterly disappoint us is the Institute for Security + Technology, who set up, with US government backing, the Ransomware Task Force, which on the face of it sounded excellent. We went all in and started discussions with their team and shared our expertise, knowledge, experience, and our desire to assist by addressing the oversight of Internet security posture. At the time, we were welcomed; however, that was soon to change. The RTF works with Palo Alto, Rapid7, Microsoft, Resilience Cyber, and the Cyber Threat Alliance, among others. The RTF released a comprehensive framework to combat Ransomware. Their website says: "The Institute for Security and Technology (IST)—in partnership with a broad coalition of experts in industry, government, law enforcement, civil society, and international organisations who participated in the Ransomware Task Force (RTF)—has released a comprehensive framework to combat Ransomware". The launch event on 29 April 2020 was well supported, and I was delighted to attend. I was a tad concerned by the near verbal and written acceptance that Ransomware attacks were here to stay, so mitigating them with Insurance, negotiation skills, and so on was highlighted, and there was very little, barely any mention in fact re prevention, which seemed crazy at the time but would become even more concerning as we started researching some of the companies involved, including the hosting company, IST.

On the weekend of 2 May, I connected with and shared our Internet security Rating screenshots for the companies involved in the inaugural RTF event with the CEO of IST, and the fact that with such poor Internet connected security results for several of the participating companies, including IST themselves. With an F and 0, not only were they prime targets for Cyber and Ransomware attacks, but such a position would also certainly call into question their advice and not inspire anyone who found such information, let alone if a Ransomware gang should find their exposed, vulnerable, and exploitable position if they were infiltrated whilst maintaining insecure positions. It was only two weeks prior that AXA declared they would no longer agree to pay ransoms as part of a cyber policy, and a week later, they had been hacked by a Ransomware attack...

I shared screenshots and intelligence with the CEO of IST and several of the attendees. I was waiting for emails of thanks, we did not know, we will look at it, address it and remediate accordingly, many thanks for highlighting these 'oversights', but nothing: not a single response from any of the several Ransomware Task Force team who were charged as thought leaders to fight against Ransomware. Some even disconnected on LinkedIn and ignored follow-up emails. What could the RTF want to achieve other than Ransomware prevention? Then it dawned upon me. Given the fact the NCSC work with RTF, maybe they had influenced RTF to overlook and ignore our findings as they had the FBI in 2020. Might the fact we are able to uncover these exposed vulnerabilities concern them so much that they try at every opportunity to dismiss, dissuade, or deny the relevance? Remember we had the NCSC report on a redacted Internet security report in 2020 which the NCSC's Technical Director Dr Ian Levy said he would be concerned, especially with the obsolete SSL, and that he would want to investigate the plethora of CVEs and other issues. It was then that I confirmed it was an NCSC subdomain and that maybe their scanning capability and tool Webchecker did not cut the mustard, clearly. Dr Ian Levy also ignored the intelligence on the Bank of England and the FCA that I shared in the previous chapter. The question must be posed knowing that the vast majority of cyberattacks, IP theft, and Ransomware attacks utilise insecure domains: Why on earth might the government not want to prevent attacks and enable security that is clearly and systemically not being achieved? The NCSC Internet security Rating is at a strong B+ and 80/100; it is only kept from being an A+ and 100 because it does not have a Content Security Policy. The NCSC has maintained a B or B+ Rating since 2017 when it was at a D and 35/100, which was pre-HTTPS wide adoption. Why might the NCSC want a strong Internet security Rating but dismiss it for others? We often use a term as we become more cynical when breaches occur, complacent or complicit.

Given our research and findings on global leaders such as MITRE CWE, Bank of England, FCA, Lloyd's, Aon, Willis, CNA, Colonial, Air India, BA, and hundreds, possibly thousands, of other companies either being breached or maintaining insecure positions, often knowingly, one must ask: Can they all be dismissing the facts and retaining insecure positions out of ignorance, lack of knowledge, and incompetence? Are cyber criminals more intelligent than the good guys, including the NCSC, the DOD, DHS, and GCHQ, or are they getting assistance? Well, possibly they are, they are unquestionably being gifted easy, unfettered access on many occasions to networks, and that includes the SolarWinds of the world. Or maybe there is a different game plan that does not include preventing any cyberattacks or Ransomware breaches. One thing is sure: there seems to be a very unpleasant taste in how, in certain quarters, the Security of Insecurity is being embraced...

16

CRITICAL NATIONAL INFRASTRUCTURE: THE COLLAPSE OF A NATION

Is America's, or indeed the world's, Critical National Infrastructure prepared for the ongoing Ransomware siege, and what can they do to avoid it? Let us come back to today, 13 May 2021. This week, we have witnessed Colonial Pipeline cyberattack, and the breach has caused a week of disruption. Gas stations and fuel lines have run dry, and a huge number of people on the East Coast are angry and want answers. The situation may only have been minimised by the restrictive travel and effects of COVID-19. Fuel prices have escalated, and Colonial have been found not to have any security worthy of note, let alone good security or good security resources. This position enabled and indeed facilitated Remote Access, and in turn, that Remote Access facilitated the breach. The total losses to Colonial this week, including the $11 million (disparate sources now suggest $4.4; however, others suggest $30 million) Ransomware payment to DarkSide, and total costs may surpass $100 million. The overall security Rating of F and 0 at Colonial is indicative of a worrying widespread and systemic position: Colonial's Internet-facing security Rating of F and 0 are as bad as ratings get, and behind this rating lies a plethora of insecure, easily exploitable, and Not Secure positions.

Apart from being a CI, what has this to do with the wider CNI and grid? The previous scenario from the future, dated December 30 2023, is fast approaching, and as part of a research program we were asked by the Energy Industry to undertake, the findings clearly indicate that unless the electric grid and CNI companies add to and severely bolster security as part of their programmes, they will in fact fall victim to these ongoing attacks and be victims, with all that will entail. We were asked to research and report on the security posture and Ratings

DOI: 10.1201/9781003278214-16

of the following providers within the sector, and the findings should act as a major wakeup call before it is simply too late. We researched the following major operators.

PJM Interconnection
MISO
ERCOT
SWPP
NE ISO
CAISO

PJM Interconnection LLC is a regional transmission organisation in the United States. It is part of the Eastern Interconnection grid operating an electric transmission system serving all or parts of Delaware, Illinois, Indiana, Kentucky, Maryland, Michigan, New Jersey, North Carolina, Ohio, Pennsylvania, Tennessee, Virginia, West Virginia, and the District of Columbia.

The Midcontinent Independent System Operator, Inc., formerly named Midwest Independent Transmission System Operator, Inc., is an independent system operator and regional transmission organization providing open-access transmission service and monitoring the high-voltage transmission system in the Midwest United States; Manitoba, Canada; and a southern United States region which includes much of Arkansas, Mississippi, and Louisiana. MISO also operates one of the world's largest real-time energy markets.

The Electric Reliability Council of Texas, Inc. is an American organisation that operates Texas's electrical grid, the Texas Interconnection, which supplies power to more than 25 million Texas customers and represents 90% of the state's electric load. ERCOT is the first independent system operator in the United States and one of nine ISOs in North America. ERCOT works with the Texas Reliability Entity, one of eight regional entities within the North American Electric Reliability Corporation that coordinate to improve reliability of the bulk power grid.

Southwest Power Pool manages the electric grid and wholesale power market for the central United States. As a regional transmission organisation, the non-profit corporation is mandated by the Federal Energy Regulatory Commission to ensure reliable supplies of power, adequate transmission infrastructure, and competitive wholesale electricity prices. Southwest Power Pool and its diverse group of member companies coordinate the flow of electricity across approximately 60,000 miles of high-voltage transmission lines spanning 14 states. The company is headquartered in Little Rock, Arkansas.

ISO-NE oversees the operation of New England's bulk electric power system and transmission lines, generated, and transmitted by its member utilities, as well as Hydro-Québec, NB Power, the New York Power Authority, and utilities in New York state when the need arises. ISO-NE is responsible for reliably operating New England's 32,000-megawatt bulk electric power generation and transmission system. One of its major duties is to provide tariffs for the prices, terms, and conditions of the energy supply in New England. The Rating of B and 75/100 is a great improvement over others and it would not be unreasonable to assume with this security Rating, ISO-NE would be the last CI on this list to be targeted.

The California Independent System Operator is a non-profit independent system operator serving California. It oversees the operation of California's bulk electric power system, transmission lines, and electricity market generated and transmitted by its member utilities. The primary stated mission of CAISO is to 'operate the grid reliably and efficiently, provide fair and open transmission access, promote environmental stewardship, and facilitate effective markets and promote infrastructure development'. The CAISO is one of the largest ISOs in the world, delivering 300 million megawatt-hours of electricity each year and managing about 80% of California's electric flow.

The addition of a homepage demonstrating it is sub optimal and Not Secure in the address bar is in the security world a cardinal sin. By using obsolete SSL/TLS certificates, the organisation effectively renders the domain owner, the company, totally exposed to cyberattacks such as Waterholes, drive-bys, shadow sites, lack of data integrity, and data stored as plaintext ready to be exfiltrated and encrypted as part of the Ransomware cycle. Given the research and findings, and the fact that the security Ratings of all but one of these critical infrastructure organisations are sub optimal, many identical at F, the same Rating as Colonial, which has been shown to have been the root cause for the initial targeting and cyberattack, we can only hypothesise how many of these companies will fall foul of similar attacks and what disruption such attacks and subsequent outages might have. One thing for sure is Ransomware attacks have become big business. Cyber gangs do not care how much disruption they cause; in fact, the more the better, as it increases the likelihood of ransoms being paid more swiftly.

Colonial Pipeline's cyberattack and subsequent decision to shut down the pipelines for several reasons, one being they were unsure how they would invoice due to the systems being down, clearly is a wake-up call that has hopefully awakened some of these sleeping and highly insecure Goliaths. Every organisation must now take security seriously; failing to do so is nothing short of being complacent and complicit. Buying a cyber policy will not be a get-out-of-jail-free card as Cyber Insurance providers become savvier; they may, and undoubtedly should, deny any settlement if, like Colonial, security was negligent and basic security was omitted.

The previous picture is dire and demonstrates a total lack of basic security across this sample group. If the same intelligence were discovered by cyber criminals, I would seriously suspect that attacks were already in flight. ... Ask the question of your Board: When is NOW a good time to address security? No matter what has gone before, security is the responsibility of every company, and the clock is ticking. Such attacks on websites and servers are at the rate of 200,000 a day. Playing Russian roulette (no pun intended) should not be a game of choice. ... The law is changing. One can outsource pretty much everything—website development, website hosting, technology management, and so on—but no one can outsource accountability and responsibility.

Would it be too hard to imagine that a Cyber Insurance provider is infiltrated due to being insecure at the Internet and then accessed and in turn breached due to their own insecure positions, the difference being the criminal now has inside intelligence on levels and agreements in place and makes demands that fit those criteria and in turn their customers' PII data, and so on? Of course not, and that is already happening at CNA, who were breached earlier this year for being insecure and maintaining an Internet security Rating of F and 0. As of writing this paragraph on 26 May 2021, I can confirm that Colonial maintain a totally insecure F and 0 Internet-connected security Rating, and CNA have slightly improved from their F and 0 to a D and 30. In both cases, the reality is both are totally open to further infiltration and breaches, and that is before we even consider what malicious plants may or may not have been planted in a similar way to

SolarWinds, and that manipulated the system for over nine months before being discovered literally by chance.

Being candid for a moment, unless we start adopting proper security, not just lip service or enough to buy cover by using a veil instead of robust, fit-for-purpose security, which, by the way, only requires discipline and expertise, everyone might just as well throw in the towel. I fear many have already. I wonder how long it will be until those responsible for 'allowing' such basic security measures to be overlooked and ignored are found to have actually done so for financial gain and to fuel the next influx of major breaches. We are dealing with criminals here; they do not care about the lives of thousands, even hundreds of thousands, even millions, of lives. They have their motive, financial, religious, or whatever, and they will do whatever it takes to achieve their objectives, and that will include bribery, corruption, and even taking lives.

Which part of this is not being understood is often a question that we ponder and think deeply about, and then we are informed of several more Ransomware attacks...

17
US State Attacks and the Continued Oversight of Security

In this chapter, we are going to look at some of the US states that have recently been victims of Ransomware attacks. We will be listing several, along with overviews, and conclude with each of their current digital security positions where they are connected to the Internet today, post breach.

Tulsa, Oklahoma, is the second-largest city in the state and the forty-seventh largest city in the United States. The population is just over 400,000. The Tulsa metropolitan area has a population close to 1 million. Originally, Tulsa was founded as a strong energy sector; however, more laterally Tulsa has more diversified sectors, including, finance, aviation, telecommunications, and technology. Tulsa has two major universities and for most of the 20th century had the nickname Oil Capital of the World. Tulsa has been and is still considered a key city.

Several weeks ago, Tulsa was hit by a Ransomware attack which saw many of their computer systems shut down, and officials warned the city that systems would be down for three to four weeks. This meant normal, everyday interaction with the state would be dramatically affected, all the way to residents paying bills, compounding the City's financial challenges and tasks further. The attack over a weekend affected the city government's network and brought down official websites. The attack is currently being handled by the city's IT team, who have managed to restore some of the city's websites. Many are still not secure, however. This is amazing, as insecure websites and domain connections are more than likely the root cause of the initial infiltration, as most breaches are. G.T. Bynum, the Mayor of Tulsa, said this week that the city would not pay a ransom demand but is focused on restoring their systems.

DOI: 10.1201/9781003278214-17

Atlanta is the capital of the state of Georgia. It is the thirty-seventh largest city in the United States, with a population of over 500,000. Atlanta serves as the cultural and economic centre of the Atlanta Metropolitan area. Atlanta was founded as the terminus of a major state-sponsored railroad and took its name from the Western and Atlantic Railroad local depot. During the Civil War, Atlanta was virtually burned to the ground in General William T Sherman's March to the Sea. Atlanta will always be associated with Martin Luther King, Jr., and Civil Rights.

In July 2018, Atlanta were the victims of a Ransomware attack known as SamSam on the municipal computer systems and networks, wreaking havoc on nearly every part of the city's government. Several months later, Gary Brantley, the then-newly appointed Chief Information Officer, said they were still digging out from one of the highest profile cyberattacks at the time against a US target; my, how things have changed. Atlanta suggested the ransom was not paid but spent, according to the city's officials: $2.7 million to recover and replace systems that were affected. Mr Brantley is no longer with the city office.

Alaska is by far the largest state in the United States by area. To put that into perspective, Texas, California, and Montana combined could all fit into Alaska. It is the third least-populated state. At least half the population live within the Anchorage Metropolitan area. Alaska has been inhabited by various indigenous people for thousands of years before the arrival of Europeans. The state is considered the entry point for the settlement of North America by way of the Bering land bridge. The US government bought Alaska in 1867 from Russia for $7.2 million, which is equivalent to $133 million, or $0.2 per acre. Alaska was officially made the forty-ninth state of the United States on 3 January 1959.

In our original research into the Internet security of the 50 US states in the spring of 2020, we started with Alaska and found some very concerning issues with their Internet-facing and connected security, so much so that we went further and sent a report to them. The report showed Not Secure homepages, along with servers that had no fewer than 27 CVEs, many allowing Remote Access with known common exploits. Alaska had suffered a recent cyberattack in January of 2019, and clearly, with some of the CVEs dating back to 2011, these had, and were continually being overlooked and ignored, along with being insecure at their Internet connections via their domains and subdomains.

The research we undertook lasted several months leading up to the 2020 US Presidential elections, during which time there was additional funding made available for all states in their attempt to prevent digital meddling, as happened in the 2016 elections. From the research and findings across all 50 states, not one was secure. I suspect and suggest that funding may not have been well used. In December 2020 following the elections, Alaska were victims of another cyberattack that caused further chaos, and only several weeks ago. That makes three attacks within two years and must be causing severe challenges to the state, its budgets and overall morale. Sadly, Alaska is seemingly lacking leadership and capability, as over the same period of all three attacks, their Internet connectivity has been, and remains, insecure.

Baltimore was designated as an independent city by the Constitution of Maryland in 1851 and today is the largest independent city in the United States. The population of Baltimore is just under 3 million, which makes it the twenty-first largest metropolitan area in the country. Baltimore is situated 40 miles northeast of Washington, DC, making it a principal city in the Washington-Baltimore CSA (Combined Statistical Area), with a total combined population of nearly 10 million. The Port of Baltimore was established in 1706 to support the tobacco trade, and shortly thereafter, in 1729, the town of Baltimore was officially established.

In May 2019, Baltimore suffered a cyberattack in the form of a RobinHood Ransomware attack. Baltimore became the second US city to fall victim to this Ransomware attack behind Greenville, North Carolina. All services, apart from essential services, were taken offline as a precautionary measure whilst the ransom demand for $76,280 to release the decryption keys was being considered. The attack had a severe negative effect on the government and the real estate market, as property transfers and purchases were left in limbo, unable to complete. It was proven that Baltimore was insecure and susceptible to such attacks due to its IT practices and the fact that the IT Manager was not allocated funds to purchase cyber insurance, nothing to do with not delivering basic security of course. The attack was compared to the earlier attack on Atlanta (see previously) for obvious reasons; however, the root cause was still being overlooked.

Denver is a city in the County of Denver and the largest city in the state of Colorado. It has a population of just over 700,000 and is the nineteenth largest city in the United States. Denver is named after James W. Denver, governor of the Kansas Territory between 1875 and 1882. Denver is ranked as a Beta world city by the Globalisation and World Cities Research Network. The ten-county Denver-Aurora-Lakewood, CO, Metropolitan Statistical Area has an estimated population of some 3 million. Denver was selected in 1970 to host the winter Olympics in 1976; however, in 1972, Colorado voters decided against allocating public funds to cover the costs. Instead, the 1976 Winter Olympics took place in Innsbruck in Austria.

In August 2020, Debbie Wilmot of Lafayette City was quoted as saying: 'If only we could turn back time, we would have scanned our computer network regularly and plugged the holes that tempt cyber prowlers'. The city had been the victim of a Ransomware attack and decided to pay the ransom of $45,000 to try to take back control of its network, phone systems, and email. This situation was one of several such incidents in Colorado. In February 2018, the Colorado Department of Transport were hit with a Ransomware attack. The state did not pay; however, it incurred $1.7 million to contain and recover some of the lost data. In February 2019, the Fort Collins Loveland Water District was struck by a Ransomware attack and apparently refused to pay and also incurred substantial costs. In August 2019, Regis University in Denver became a victim of another Ransomware attack. It paid an undisclosed sum to the ransom gang. In December 2019, Aurora Water were hit with a cyberattack via their vendor Click2Gov. In April 2020, Rangley District Hospital fell victim to yet another Ransomware attack and as usual had data encrypted, including patient health records and PII data. The hospital said it did not pay the ransom. In April 2020, the Parkview Medical Centre was also hit with a Ransomware attack which closed their website. Foolishly, the Centre said it would not affect patients... In June 2020, Children's Hospital Colorado's systems and emails had been accessed, and it notified 255 patients of the compromise. The list continues, as it does in all states and cities within this chapter, and the sad thing is no one has addressed the root cause and continue to maintain insecure domains connected to the Internet.

Knoxville is a tad smaller as a city to the others in this listing; however, with a population of nearly 200,000, it is nonetheless a significant city in Knox County in Tennessee. Knoxville is the third-largest city in the East Tennessee Grand Division, behind Nashville and Memphis. The first settlers in Knoxville were in 1786, and the arrival of the railroad in 1855 led to an economic boom. The Civil War bitterly divided the region. Following the war, Knoxville grew rapidly as a major wholesaling and manufacturing centre. In 1982, Knoxville hosted the World's Fair, which helped reinvigorate the city. The University of Tennessee is based in Knoxville, as is Tennessee's supreme court.

According to Knox News, Knoxville received a demand of $393,137 to enable them to retrieve their data from the attackers; however, they refused to pay. The attackers had attacked Knoxville with DopplePaymer Ransomware, which had infiltrated, exfiltrated, and then encrypted the data. This has become the default sequence of events in Ransomware attacks. Kristen Farley, the city's communications director, said that the groups the city hired to investigate the 11 June attack had completed their work and had identified the compromised accounts and planned to mail several hundred letters to the affected parties. Knox News went on to explain that cyberattacks on local governments are not uncommon. They can begin when an employee opens a bogus email that appears legitimate and enters a username and password, allowing cybercriminals access to the computer system. Knox are correct to an extent; however, all of this, including a Phishing email campaign, is certainly easier and more acceptable if a server via an insecure website is first accessed and utilised making the Phishing emails look like internal emails as happened to the FBI towards the end of 2021. In fact, total Domain Admin Access can be obtained via this route, as in last December's SolarWinds cyberattack that affected some 18,000 companies. Breaches can be like an incredibly long line of stacked dominoes: push one over and you can sit back and watch the rest fall…

New Orleans is world renowned for its distinctive music and is located along the Mississippi River in the southeastern region of Louisiana. New Orleans has a population of around 400,000, the largest population in the region. New Orleans is known as an economic and commercial hub for the Gulf Coast in the United States. New Orleans is considered a unique city in the United States due to its diverse culture, cuisine, and music. New Orleans was originally founded in 1718 by French colonists before being purchased by the United States in 1803. In 1840, New Orleans was the US's third-largest city by population. The city has been vulnerable to flooding due to its high rainfall and low-lying position, poor drainage, and location near multiple bodies of water. New Orleans was severely affected by Hurricane Katrina in August 2005, which flooded more than 80% of the city. Since Katrina, major developments have seen a major rebound in the region's population, investments, and economic future.

In late 2019, New Orleans were hit by a Ransomware attack that followed a similar attack on the state of Louisiana. Mayor LaToya Cantrell declared a state of emergency. The attack started on Friday 13 December 2019. All systems were shut down under the city's NOLA Cyber Security defence program, as literally all government employees were told to unplug their devices and disconnect from the Wi-Fi. It was confirmed that the city's cameras were still recording, so incident footage could be used if required. Fire and police departments were able to respond to phone calls. Only weeks prior to this attack, the FBI had alerted local governments, states, and cities of increased cyberattack activity, especially against healthcare, commerce, and transportation. There had been two major breaches in the United States within the transportation sector. This attack followed an earlier attack in November against the state of Louisiana. On 23 August 2020, government agencies were taken offline by a cyberattack in the state of Texas. Without question, US municipalities were in the firing line and being targeted. Of course, it is easy to believe what the motive may be; however, the obvious root cause is constantly being overlooked time after time. Because of that oversight, the root cause remains vulnerable, exposed, and exploitable after $millions, quite possibly hundreds of $millions have been wasted, and it is not easy to understand why.

Unequivocally, Ransomware gangs are now more brazen than ever, along with increasing ransom demands and payments. Look at CNA's confirmation of a $40 million ransom payment recently. As part of their reconnaissance using OSINT technology, cybercriminals identify insecure organisations, and then by gaining access, they can infect the network of larger metropolitan areas and those connected to it. The trend has also been to exfiltrate some readily available plain text data to prove they have gained access and by doing so, under whatever privacy laws are in place requiring the security of personal identifiable information (PII), the breach also falls foul of local privacy laws, too, resulting in fines and potentially Class Action Lawsuits.

Most people do not understand, and sadly, that incredibly seems to include far too many security professionals and regulators. When a website is easily compromised by being misconfigured, insecure, or using obsolete SSL digital certificates, the data at rest and in flight (transit) can be in plain text. All data should and must be encrypted; it is a main security feature. The fact it can be accessed in plain text makes data incredibly attractive to cybercriminals, as they can then exfiltrate plain text data, then encrypt it and leverage their position for a ransom payment. In truth, it is a security cardinal sin to enable digital certificates to expire or be misconfigured when websites rely upon them for security, and yet even Microsoft are caught napping in this area. That fact (or excuse) does not reduce the impact or make it acceptable or less destructive. However, websites are scanned for vulnerabilities by cyber criminals at the rate of 200,000 per day, that is, 8,333 websites an hour or 138 websites scanned every minute of every day for vulnerabilities, and when they are found, attacks are launched.

It naturally follows that if a website is insecure, uses obsolete SSL certificates, is misconfigured, harbours numerous CVEs, and so on, the chances of infiltration from an attack being launched in the first place are significantly higher than a secure one and then can go unnoticed. The direct correlation between Internet insecurity, number of websites, and number of successful cyberattacks, including Ransomware, is no coincidence.

In July 2019, the US Conference of Mayors unanimously passed a resolution calling on local officials to cease paying Ransomware demands to cybercriminal gangs who were taking over their networks. However, despite that resolution, many cities, including some of those mentioned previously, have paid ransom demands after being faced with losing important data or after Ransomware gangs threatened to leak sensitive user data on the dark web. We extensively researched all of these cities and many of the states as part of our comprehensive 50 US state research pre the 2020 US Presidential elections and found a systemic security failing across all states. Not one had an acceptable security position, which our full report demonstrates and supports.

Until agencies and governments change their position and continue to nullify and ignore the critical importance of Internet security, cyberattacks and Ransomware attacks will continue unabated. The frequency and scale of attacks will simply continue to increase. A year and a half ago, at the beginning of 2020, when we found Travelex, who had been hacked, were running obsolete SSL on their homepage that led to the identification of their insecure position and then infiltration, I would receive one, maybe two, breach alerts every few days; now I get two to three every day. It is already too late for many, as is the fact that due to negligence of security, every adult, and more who are resident in the United States, most probably have had their PII data illegally taken, many several times. This includes all military and agency staff, partly due to the OPM breach in 2015 and continuous, ongoing daily assaults globally, with, as mentioned, around 80% against the United States.

Oversight, negligence, complacency or even complicit behaviour, it is hard to say which caused the position we are in today; however, what we do know is unless governments start driving an urgent, planet-scale change, with the likes of Ransomware Task Forces, cyber security groups and companies, government, agencies, and all organisations actually taking their own security and that of others where they are connected to the Internet via their websites seriously, you might as well start looking for a deserted island to live on, as the world is currently in freefall due to cybercrime. Forget the fact our governments originally designed and developed the methods and techniques being used against us daily; they now need to stand and be counted instead of making false accusations of sophisticated and state-backed attacks. The position they have created will and already possibly is affecting every person in the world, and they must ultimately be held to account; two wrongs will never make a right. ... As President Ronald Reagan said, 'The scariest words in the English language are; I'm from the government, and I'm here to help'.

18

Conflicts of Interest

'Cyberattacks do not cost enough in terms of financially or loss of lives'
a Leading Security expert from the Ministry of Defence said to me in
a meeting in 2019, and sadly, he was right. He also confirmed that the
MOD desperately required our services, as they had no idea whatsoever
what devices they had, let alone the sheer billions of digital certificates
they had across those devices and the network. He was also very familiar with the 'use' of digital certificates by GCHQ and their US counter-
parts over the years, which had played a role but were as much a liability
now as they were useful. He then introduced me to Fujitsu, as the 'contracts' worth hundreds of £millions would need to go through them.

The Academy of the MOD suffered a cyberattack in the spring of
2021 and research proved their, and Fujitsu's basic security was woeful at best, along with Serco's who ultimately took the blame for the
intrusion.

A meeting was set up with Fujitsu's MOD technical and security
team, and several PoCs (Proofs of Concept) were agreed and were to
be set up. Discussions on costs took place, and Fujitsu confirmed they
wanted PoCs for free. Knowing the potential 'size of the prize', we
agreed with restrictions and awaited dates. It was at this point Fujitsu
went AWOL. Totally off the radar, did not respond, as they had previously, to emails and calls. Fujitsu and effectively the MOD had firmly
closed their doors without any PoC even though they fully comprehended the capability and uniqueness of our technology. Fujitsu are
currently facing widespread calls for accountability for their role in
the long-term debacle of their software Horizon and the glitches that
caused the wrong criminal cases to be brought against 900 Post Masters. Horizon cost the government some £1 billion, was flawed from
its conception, and created the UK's worst miscarriage of justice. All
Post Office Masters have been subsequently vindicated; however, it has
taken over 25 years, many have died and many been made bankrupt

DOI: 10.1201/9781003278214-18

and had their lives negatively impacted due to Horizons and Fujitsu's failings. The Post Office, the UK government, and Fujitsu have yet to apologise, and all those incorrectly convicted now have the additional challenge to seek compensation—a very dark day in the history of the UK government's handling and procurement capabilities along with highly questionable Law practices.

I can only speculate at this point; however, the reality is although Whitethorn as a technology is unrivalled and had originally been developed to discover 'Stuxnet'-style compromised digital certificates within a NATO military installation following a cyberattack and breach. The breach resulted in highly sensitive data being made available on the Dark Web (the only reason a breach was identified). Although the unique capabilities of our technology were appreciated; however, I believe the powers that be also realised that the technology would undoubtedly uncover, and disclose, the plethora of 'Plants' the agencies and governments had themselves and indeed had placed elsewhere, given that we found Flying Pig GCHQ digital certificates within one of the Big 4 Accounting firms whilst undertaking a PoC. It would also show the incredible level and lack of controls at the government providers as well as the MOD and government. Best sweep it away and deny the problem.

Let us not be naïve. It is well known that many, indeed all, major organisations have people that are known as DHs ('Double Hatters'). A DH does their day job; they also ensure intelligence is fed back to the Mothership. In the United Kingdom, that is GCHQ and in the United States the NSA or similar. In most cases, the companies are fully aware and accommodate such positions for their own benefit and, again, for certain sanctions and government contracts. It certainly does not mean security is improved in any way, shape, or form; however, the agencies may have a different view. Nonetheless, when dealing with security in major organisations, do not be fooled into thinking the CSO/CISO make decisions; they will often seek sanction from the Mothership when push comes to shove and especially when it comes to unprecedented capabilities and visibility within a network. Remember, since 9/11, the agencies wanted to achieve digital dominance and control and stopped at nothing to achieve it and achieve it they did. Make no mistake, when I finish writing this chapter, along with all the others, if I emailed it on a regular email, it can easily and will be intercepted, and long before this book is published, certain people in certain government organisations would have had the chance to read it...

Digital data mass collection was fully disclosed several years ago and was possibly rated as one of the world's worst-kept secrets. It is no coincidence most tech giants are US based or that most emails and communication are routed one way or another via the United States. That is all well and good; however, as I have said, and confirmed repeatedly, the same methods of mass data capture and mass data collection methods, along with harvesting capability have formed what is now known as Cyberattacks and Ransomware. It has yet to be proven exactly who are the cybercriminals really are; however, given the lack of defensive capabilities, it often feels like own goals are being scored across many sectors and on many occasions.

When the US government recently set up and gave $111 million to a university to educate the US manufacturing sector how to better protect themselves and yet the university is totally open to a cyberattack due to using obsolete SSL digital certificate and has a security Rating of F, one has to question exactly what the manufacturing sector is going to learn...

Equally, as we touched on in a previous chapter, the newly formed Ransomware Task Force, backed by the DHS and supported by the NCSC, and yet five of the six, including the RTF body themselves, are maintaining F-Rated Internet-connected domains along with woeful security. One must question the leadership and messages being educated and passed onto more unsuspecting and unknowing companies. The phrase 'blind leading the blind' springs to mind. Is this mass and gross incompetence or mass facilitation? It is easy to be confused and find major issues with the current lack of security. When we emailed information and shared screenshots of the positions to these organisations showing their insecure positions, the response was from being ignored to being disconnected on LinkedIn after reviewing the information and doing nothing to remediate their position. 'Do as we say, not as we do' is alive and kicking.

Recently Mersey Rail in the UK was the latest of a group of travel and rail organisations to be subjected to a cyberattack and breach. As soon as the news broke, we researched, and as usual, found a raft of security failings and the normal F and 0-Rated Internet-connected domains. We notified them immediately, along with their CEO. We emailed several connected organisations, including the Department of Transport, who coincidentally today just emailed me their response to my original email of 4 May 2021, three weeks ago. The response is as follows:

Department
for Transport

Department for Transport
Great Minster House
33 Horseferry Road
London
SW1P 4DR
Tel: 0300 330 3000

Web Site: www.gov.uk/dft

Our Ref: 341725

28 May 2021

Andrew Jenkinson

andrew.jenkinson@cybersecip.com

Dear Andrew Jenkinson

MerseyRail Ransomware Incident

Thank you for your email of 4 May to the Secretary of State. Your email was transferred to the cyber team and I have been asked to reply.

As you will understand, due to the ongoing investigation into the MerseyRail cyber-attack, we cannot comment on the specifics of the incident.

We are committed to reducing the risk to the UK posed by cyber-attack, by working in a joined-up way with our partners and the sector. While the cyber risks to the transport sector are largely owned and managed by the private sector, DfT's role is to provide advice and guidance with the support of the National Cyber Security Centre (NCSC), and to set the regulatory framework to help operators and owners to mitigate the risk.

One of the regulatory levers we have implemented is the Network and Information Systems (NIS) Regulation (2018). The NIS Regulations are designed to increase the security of network and information systems that support the provision of essential services within the transport sector. While it is too early to judge the long-term impact of the regulations, organisations are taking measures to ensure the security of their networks and information systems as a result of the Regulations being in place.

On ransomware, we have worked closely with NCSC on developing and promoting guidance on mitigating malware and ransomware attacks. This guidance helps organisations deal with the effects of malware (which includes ransomware). It provides actions to help organisations prevent a malware infection, and steps to take if you're already infected. The NCSC also runs a commercial scheme called Cyber Incident Response, where certified companies provide support to affected organisations.

We will continue to work with industry and partners to increase cyber security resilience in the transport sector and utilise all the levers we have available. I hope that this goes some way to addressing your concerns.

Yours sincerely

Liam Panter

DfT Cyber Policy Team

My response to Liam at the Department for Transport was very polite; however, I suggested that possibly the cyber security team and the NCSC must be too busy, as the domain connecting Mersey Rail to the Internet and to enable people to purchase tickets, plan journeys, and so on was still rated at F and 0. This Rating confirms that no one, NCSC or otherwise, had addressed the lacking critical security of Mersey Rail at the place they had been targeted, infiltrated, and been held ransom to: the Internet. At this stage, one could say: Andy, you're being harsh; there's lots going on and the panic button and alarm have been pressed and sounded. That is certainly the case; however, by default, this situation, like thousands of other breaches, are nothing short of being self-inflicted. As we have said many, many times and will never relent until it is understood: *The Internet and the Insecure connections to it by companies' domains are the root cause of and access to the majority of cyberattacks. Unless this critical area is secured, cyberattacks and ransomware attacks will continue unabated.*

Last January, easyJet suffered a cyberattack that potentially saw the PII data of some 9 million people accessed and exfiltrated. The NCSC were called in, as were a leading cyber security major player. Between the consultancy and the NCSC, it was decided to not share the information about the breach for over three months, until April 2020. We extensively researched easyJet's domains and ecosystem connected to the Internet and found numerous insecure domains with obsolete digital certificates, misconfigured certificate chains, and an Internet security Rating of F and 0. So for three months and behind closed doors, the NCSC and the major cyber security firm had time to identify the issues and make basic security improvements. In April, we shared our research and findings with easyJet themselves and the NCSC. We got little to no response so set up a call with Stelios, easyJet's main shareholder, who was unimpressed with the current board of easyJet and wanted them dismissed. We continued alerting easyJet, who also notified the entire world of their breach, quite unbelievably on a Not Secure website; it was more than a farce, it was simply unbelievable.

So, here is the question: Since easyJet were breached, not complying with all UKDPA and GDPR privacy laws and regulations, and have worked with the NCSC and a leading cyber security firm, why, sixteen months later, are easyJet still maintaining F- and 0-rated domains? If someone can provide a sensible answer, I would love to hear, and that question is open to the NCSC, GCHQ, NSA, CIA, FBI, easyJet, or the specialist cyber security consulting firm. How many £millions have been spent and wasted chasing false security, whilst for nearly a year and a half, easyJet are totally insecure and continuing to break all privacy laws? If you go online today and book easyJet flights, chances are the security of their digital platforms and domains is in the exact same position as last January when they were breached via them. I would seriously question easyJet's compliance with privacy laws. These findings stimulated our wider research in the sector that proved numerous other similar companies have a very similar, if not identical, insecure position. So again, why might the NCSC, with their Internet security Rating of B+ and 80/100 and who totally understand how Internet security can be manipulated, abused, and exploited—indeed, they, along with the NSA, 'wrote the book' on such tactics—not advise companies pre or post breach to ensure they indeed have Internet security?

The situation and answers are abundantly clear. The tactics the US and UK governments and agencies used and perfected to gain mass data intelligence and infiltration in the new digital, post-cold war are considered too convenient and provide too much intelligence, so they do not want anyone to close the digital doors or even alert unsuspecting organisations or executives of their previous antics. Think of it in a similar way to the major tobacco companies refuting the fact that smoking caused cancer for decades following the findings by German scientists in the 1920s and further demonstrable evidence in the United Kingdom in the 1950s. The industry fought against the truth in terms of denial both publicly and in legal battles. Interestingly, rates of consumption since 1965 in the developed world either peaked or declined; however, they continue to climb in the developing world. Pretty much everyone acknowledges and knows smoking is bad for you; however, hundreds of millions of intelligent people ignore the massive signs confirming the dangers and smoke. Furthermore, the revenues and taxes today are readily accepted by governments worldwide, knowing that the trade-off will be much higher Healthcare costs and reduction of life expectancy. Governments often look at short-term gains and ignore long-term challenges, and that is exactly what happened, by default or by design, we are unclear, with the US and UK governments and agencies so far as the manipulation of the digital world and Internet, it will be someone else's problem.

Are we too late to do anything about it? I believe that the agencies are straightening their ties in their grey suits, puffing up their chests, and hoping that deterrence theory will save their backsides. Their bullish tactics and the conflict of interest they have, and the one that they created, are at a crossroads. Ransomware attacks occur several times a day within governments, healthcare, commerce, education—pretty much every attack uses the very same tactics that our governments designed, developed, and perfected. They are loath to tell the truth and instead blame sophisticated attacks by Nation State–backed cyber criminals and are then called in to oversee the situation. The previous letter from the DfT closes with the following:

> We will continue to work with Industry and partners (NCSC) to increase cyber security resilience in the transport sector and utilise all the levers we have available. I hope that this goes some way to addressing your concerns.

Sadly, it does absolutely nothing to address any concerns or remediate the woefully insecure position of this, easyJet, or any other organisation that our government are called in to assist. Is it a major cyber breach cover-up and continued access to hundreds of millions of companies by governments? Remember the comment by the MOD: 'Cyberattacks do not cost enough in terms of financially or loss of lives'. Well, that is all changing, as we witness daily…

19

INNOVATION AND DISBELIEF

Innovation is often challenged long before it is accepted, and Infosec, cyber security, and basic security are currently going through the mill. Companies are being created as unicorns, with governments lining up to buy from them because another department did, only to find they have all been breached because not one of them ever bothered to check if the unicorn was itself secure and frequently isn't.

Let us look at some of the innovations that changed the world that were initially ridiculed and dismissed long before ever being accepted. The first of these is Thomas Edison's light bulb.

Thomas Edison is revered as the father of inventions. Edison patented no less than 1093 designs and methods in the United States alone. When Edison was known to be developing what would turn out to be the world's first electric light bulb, he faced mass ridicule. The British government were noted as saying in 1878 that the invention may be good enough for our transatlantic friends but not worthy of the attention of practical or scientific men. A senior Post Office executive said that the subdivision of the electric light was nothing more than a fairy tale. As we know, the electric light bulb has unquestionably revolutionised the worlds' ability to utilise light 24 × 7 for nearly 150 years…

Coffee today is almost a daily ritual for billions of people and possibly the most-consumed beverage and has created multi-$billion industries. The comment 'I cannot do anything worth doing before I have had my first coffee' will resonate with many. However, it was not always that way. In the 1500s, coffee was shunned for many reasons. It was considered to induce a state of drunkenness, and places where coffee was consumed were considered centres for reactionaries. It was also considered to cause several common diseases. Coffee had been made popular by Sufi Muslims to stay awake during their night-time devotions. Today coffee shops account for a large percentage of high street premises and employ millions of people globally.

DOI: 10.1201/9781003278214-19

For many years, manned flight was tried and resulted in fatalities. In 1903, the Wright Brothers made headlines for the world's first-ever manned flight that lasted 12 seconds. In the First World War, Ferdinand Foch stated in 1911 that airplanes were interesting but only as scientific toys; they had no military value. In 1919, Foch had changed his tune and stated that the Curtiss seaplane that had crossed the Atlantic Ocean from Newfoundland to Portugal was the future and that wars were won with the proven success of the military planes. The Second World War was fought extensively in the air, the Battle of Britain made into films, and the stunning Spitfire applauded globally for playing a vital part of bringing the Second World War to an end.

Today, COVID-19 aside, hundreds of thousands of airplanes transport billions of people around the world and enrich their lives. The Travel Industry was revolutionised by the advent of passenger planes, and the industry not only provides work for millions of people, it also generates revenues in the hundreds of $billions—a far cry from a 12-second flight that two brothers committed their life's work to all those years ago.

In the 1750s, Jonas Hanway, a British man, was seen using a new device called an umbrella that he had acquired in France. The lighter version, a lady's parasol, had been used for some time and accepted; however, Jonas was seen to bring the whole gender issue into question and rotten vegetables and rubbish were hurled at him whilst he attempted to stay dry (well, it was the United Kingdom). It was decades before the gender gap issue diminished and the much-needed 'brolly' was accepted for both genders to benefit from.

A big one is personal computers. In a 1996 book called *Women and Computers*, it was stated that women were afflicted with 'Computerphobia', a panoply of conditions that reflected the fear of touching or damaging a computer. It went further and cited a fear and aversion to touching, damaging, discussing, or becoming proficient with a PC. The book concluded that women were fearful of becoming addicted to a PC, who would ever have thought it. The term 'computerphobia' had sprung up in many publications of the day, including *The Atlantic*. PCs were seen and treated with a certain degree of pessimism and considered something of a chore to learn and master, now few things are ever undertaken without one.

It would not be unreasonable to say that today, a few short decades after the original scepticism, the entire world relies upon computing and PCs. Countries, taxes, purchases, infrastructure, banks, governments—literally without exception, every single thing we do, and use relies on computers. The Computing Industry is one of the largest sectors in the world today and accounts for many of the world's richest companies. Could you think of a world without computers today? Of course not, as they touch our lives every day. We will dive into that further at the end of this chapter.

When the first taxis came into being in the early 1900s, anyone could become a taxi driver, such as ex-convicts and people with questionable habits and traits. It was not until 1907, when Harry N. Allen, a 30-year-old businessman, was charged $5 for a three-quarter mile ride in Manhattan (nearly $150 today), that he decided to buy a fleet of 65 French Darracq taxi cabs all in red and hired drivers for them to create the world's first taxi fleet. At that time, only the well-heeled could afford taxis; however, Allen's new taxis ceased opaque charging to make taxis more affordable. When the taxi medallion system was rolled out in New York in 1937, the local government began regulating taxis and their drivers. In New York alone (pre COVID-19), around 400,000 taxi journeys are made, which is twice the number of Uber and Lyft journeys combined. Taxis and shared rides (pooled and fractional ownership) have revolutionised local travel, and that is before we start the next journey of electric, semi- and fully autonomous vehicles. Such situations rely on technology and innovation, and currently there are major challenges ensuring control without digital intervention. Single-use digital certification and a Zero Trust Architectures are a must and yet are nowhere near possible due to the issues we have addressed previously with PKI and the issuance, control, and management of digital certificates.

This subject of vaccinations is very current. A smallpox outbreak in the 1870s led to a call for a vaccination program. A group of anti-vaccinationists (anti-vaxxers now) campaigned heavily against such a program. Nothing particularly new; however, the main bone of contention was the law stating immunisation was required. It was argued that personal hygiene and bodily control would provide the freedom of choice to enable opting out of state-mandated vaccinations. In a Boston court in the early 1870s, an anti-vaxxer fought the law through local and supreme courts to remain unvaccinated. He lost both cases, and sometime later, as we know, smallpox was globally eradicated in the 1980s. Global public health considers vaccination programmes crucial to advance general health and fight viruses.

Today, as we know it is generally acknowledged, medicine is a critical part of the public's overall health. The Pharmaceutical Industry is a vast sector and, in the main, develops many major drugs that change comfort and address diseases accordingly. $billions are spent annually on research and development to better improve the globe's health and population. Sadly, the Pharmaceutical Industry is also one of the most targeted sectors as far as cybercrime and attacks are concerned. There are two main reasons that this Industry, as well as healthcare in general, suffer badly: 1) they have people's lives at stake, which focuses the mind more than anything, and with long-term research taking years and costing $billions, the size of the prize is considered too valuable to allow attacks and exfiltration, which encourages ransom payments, and 2) both the Pharmaceutical and the healthcare industries are systemically poor at achieving and controlling even the very basic security and by doing so, make themselves easy targets.

We covered in an earlier chapter the NSA and GCHQ's desire to dominate and control the digital world and the Internet and how that led to total capture of all data: at rest, and in flight, no matter where or how it was stored or kept. The NSA and GCHQ designed and developed comprehensive, and in many cases very smart, technology to capture and digitally eavesdrop on every man, woman, and child using any digital device anywhere in the world and in essence, succeeded in doing so. The challenge is although they had a major head start, the original control they had has been rebalanced, and what was once a monopoly on data capture, infiltration, and exfiltration is now available literally to anyone who is happy to break the law.

We constantly alert organisations to the fact that the Internet is being used by their organisation all day, every day, and if it is connected by websites that are insecure or, even worse, showing as Not Secure in the address bar, not only have they made themselves a target, but they can be, and more than likely will be, easily infiltrated. An insecure website might look secure but be insecure, as our Fs and 0s show day in day out; however, there is no hiding when the address bar says Not Secure.example.com.

The NSA and GCHQ will not discuss or confirm many of their programmes and activities; however, both know of the critical importance of Internet security, as both make sure they have it and have abused possibly millions of others by infiltrating their websites. The challenge they face is the position the world is in that sooner or later, they, governments, and incompetent security professional leaders who continue wasting $billions on false security and still get breached will finally realise the only area left, the area they have all ignored for decades, is the security of Internet domain connections. The sad truth is the tools developed within the OSINT sector were designed and developed to aid vulnerability testing and remediation, just as moving from HTTP to HTTPS was an effort to improve security; in both cases, all they have managed to do. However, because of mass incompetence, it also enables cybercriminals to identify those organisations that are vulnerable and insecure more easily to launch attacks. Organised criminals are better organised than those tasked and paid, often well, to ensure security. History will show that organisations such as ours and people like my incredible, dedicated, and unwavering team have been trying to educate the general public, and far too many so-called experts and executives, on the errors of their ways and the unbelievable, foolish mistakes that have been made through lack of knowledge or being encouraged and influenced incorrectly by the very same people who have manipulated the creators of the challenges we all face today, which then lead to further cyberattacks and Ransomware breaches.

Stop, look, listen to what you are doing and start realising the foolishness of your actions. You do not have to be incompetent, complacent, or even complicit, as that will not help you when you're breached or even in the dock facing criminal charges for conspiracy and negligence.

20

BLACKBAUD, CYBERATTACKS, AND CLASS ACTION LAWSUITS

Blackbaud is a Cloud provider that serves charity, not-for-profit, foundation, education, and healthcare organisations predominantly. Blackbaud's flagship is a fundraising SQL product called Raisers Edge. It lists its services as fundraising, website management (we will look at this further in the chapter), CRM, analytics, financial management, and education administration. Blackbaud was founded in 1981 by Anthony Bakker and is headquartered in Daniel Island, Charleston, South Carolina.

In 1994, Blackbaud converted its software offerings from DOS to Windows 95. That decision saw sales increase from $19 million to $25 million in 1996. During this time, Blackbaud was acquiring numerous DOS competitors within the sector, including ACOMS, PINOLE, and Master Software, the last acquisition doubled Blackbaud's customer base. Blackbaud started adding resellers to the business in 1998 and completed its IPO in 2004. With a flurry of activity and ex-Cap Gemini and Microsoft senior executives taking the helm, Blackbaud looked to be in great shape with a successful business model and satisfied customers in a niche marketplace. Acquisitions continued, and in 2014, Blackbaud acquired MicroEdge for $160 million and a year later, in 2017, completed the acquisition of JustGiving for £95 million. In 2018, the acquisitions continued with the purchase of Reeher for $40 million, and in 2019, they acquired YourCase, a SaaS (Software as a Service) provider.

In May 2020, Blackbaud were the victims of a cyberattack. Initially, Blackbaud played down the effects from the attack; however, customer data was stolen, and Blackbaud decided it was easier to pay the ransom demand. Interestingly, although Blackbaud is a publicly

DOI: 10.1201/9781003278214-20

traded company listed on the NASDAQ exchange and has a market cap of $2.7 billion due to revenues of just under $1 billion and would have to complete a Form 8-K with the SEC should it want to include the ransom paid in their financials, a Blackbaud spokesperson at the time said they would not be filing an 8-K form.

The cyberattack was far reaching, and quite possibly the full extent is still being discovered. However, what we do know is the customers affected by their breach had knock-on consequential implications and adversities, including over 20 universities and dozens of charities across the United States, United Kingdom, and Canada. Even our own Bletchley Park succumbed to a consequential attack and at the time said the costs might be so extensive and prohibitive they would have to close the home of British Intelligence and the home of Alan Turing and the Enigma team due to Blackbaud's cyberattack.

As with all these events, it is critical that liabilities be addressed, and with over 120 organisations adversely affected, such events and closures could take many years to finally settle. A question that we embarked upon immediately following the breach at Blackbaud was announced was: Were Blackbaud securely connected to the Internet? As a company, and as mentioned in the first paragraph previously, Blackbaud sold their services, and among these was website management. No matter whom you talk to, on, or off the record, at the NCSC, NSA, CIA, or any technology intelligence-based agency, website security is critical. The most we got the NSA to publish earlier this year was their paper based on our continued campaign concerning how Obsolete TLS digital certificates could cause vulnerabilities and exposures that could be exploited, and although the NSA published it, the content and intent were very much one of our initiatives. It could equally have been one of our documents and echoed everything we had stated for years.

We undertook research on Blackbaud's Internet-facing security, and, although shocking, we are no longer shocked, as we have sadly come to expect security incompetence and negligence. Blackbaud's homepage was scanned on 25 November 2019 and showed F and 0 security Ratings. It was scanned again on 19 July and showed security Ratings of D− and 25. It was further scanned on 21 August 2020 and showed security Ratings of F and 20. Leading up to and including the period in which Blackbaud had been targeted and breached, they maintained insecure Internet connectivity with the worst possible security Ratings, which means several insecure positions were being maintained. Interestingly, after the breach and once someone alerted them to their position—it could have been one of our emails to their CEO Michael Gianoni—Blackbaud improved their Internet security and by 30 December had improved their Internet security Rating to a C and 55 and improved it even further, when tested recently on 1 May 2021, to a B and 75. It currently sits at a C and 55. This research and findings demonstrate two things: first, Internet security fluctuates, sometimes quite dramatically, and second, Blackbaud were breached during their poorest Internet security scores. … We are not on the inside; however, such research and findings are not an exception; they are the norm. In fact, I would go so far as to say that we have never researched any organisation that was breached that had an A+ Rating with a 100 score. Without exception, they have all been an F and low score or sometimes a Rating of a D with 25 score due to Cross-Site Scripting, lack of HSTS, or similar. There can be any one of a dozen or more reasons, and cyber criminals need just one.

Now it is time for the Legal guys to start dissecting the sequence of events and try to apportion blame, and hopefully not just have the victim, though usually found guilty of being reckless, at fault, lacking duty of care, and negligent, for lessons to be learned. Unfortunately, sometimes the awful taste of the medicine is required for a patient to truly benefit. Sadly, this is rarely the case in the world of security. One only has to look at Marriott and Equifax's current poor Internet security Ratings to realise they have learned very little, even though I have shared intelligence with their CEOs and Executives. It never fails to amaze me that companies will be more prepared to give audience to and pay the bad guys attacking them and holding them to ransom than they are to give an audience to the good guys trying to alert them with Actionable Intelligence. It is nothing short of the definition of insanity, and they learn very little—complacent or complicit…

One of the plaintiffs suing Blackbaud is Heidi Imhof of Tampa, Florida, who filed a Class Action Lawsuit against Blackbaud in federal court after she learned her personally identifiable information had been captured during a cyberattack on Blackbaud. Imhof says Blackbaud should be held liable for allowing the data breach and for waiting months to inform its customers of the incident. We are in total agreement with her, so much so that we have reached out to Heidi to offer our services and share our research and findings, all of which is screenshotted and catalogued for such instances. Imhof herself was written to by Stetson University on 2 October alerting her to the fact her PII data was possibly compromised due to the fact that Stetson was a Blackbaud customer.

It is a very sad state of affairs that organisations such as Blackbaud are happy to sell their security and web services all while being Not Secure themselves, sound familiar? Little to no due diligence by university after university, charity after charity, organisation after organisation, and the domino was pushed and the rest toppled by the negligence of the Blackbaud security team. We have had our eyes opened recently with some work we are doing with the European Risk Institute and now never rule out insider collusion, money laundering, and fraud. If a company like Sony can collude with criminals and pay a $50 million ransom, that is a lot of money that could be distributed among many. When did you last hear of a bank robbery of $50 million in cash? Exactly, however, in the digital world, Ransomware attacks and payments are witnessing $billions being paid—or is it being laundered? Less we forget, these figures are daily, and unless Internet security, known as the gateway for cybercriminal access, is addressed and vastly improved, the ongoing losses will continue, and no doubt increase and become more frequent. We are witnessing the world's most toxic and detrimental economic and monetary shift to criminals that do not care about others' lives, mass destruction, and deprivation. It is not a world they live in, and it is being fuelled, funded, and supported by the likes of negligent companies such as the Blackbaud's of the world.

It is also worth noting that most customers of Blackbaud are also guilty of maintaining insecure positions. Last year we undertook a full research program across all of higher Education (universities) in the United States, including the Ivy League, and the findings clearly demonstrated sub optimal security and a plethora of Not Secure domains. As we know, numerous universities and colleges are targeted and breached frequently. Everyone is reporting breaches at alarming rates; however, we are possibly the only company in the world that provides evidence of why and how such organisations are targeted in the first place and then easily breached. So the wheels go around and around.

We recently undertook a PoC within the Education Sector here in the United Kingdom. The findings were very similar and a major cause for concern. Letters to the Secretary of State go unaddressed, and even when responded to by a junior, the content is more verbal diarrhoea that has no context, as they lean heavily on and point to the NCSC, who in turn do nothing to remediate for fear of the mask and veils being lifted from their previous and ongoing antics. It would appear they, along with the governments, are more than happy to allow cyberattacks and breaches to occur, as their actions speak a lot louder than the deafening silence...

Furthermore, if the ICO in the United Kingdom is funded by fines being levied, they need a new business model. Everyone knows they are most definitely not independent and work hand in glove with the government and agencies, slapping the occasional wrist to make it look as if they are performing the job properly. BA were totally negligent and insecure due to lacking Internet security, controls, and management, like thousands of others. Many months later, a fine was issued of £128 million. It was vastly reduced months later to £20 million, whilst the government, that is, the British taxpayer, lends BA £500 million. You could not make this up, and it makes a total mockery of the thousands of security professionals working tirelessly in vain attempts to provide security with their eyes covered and hands tied behind their backs.

The government and their so-called intelligence agencies must also be held to account. Do not get me wrong: companies are being totally and grossly negligent, either by design or default, and allowing attacks and breaches to occur; however, the government and their agencies are doing nothing more than paying lip service to the systemic challenges and taking next to no action to improve the dire situation other than telling the Education sector to place a memo in their handbooks to be vigilant, as Ransomware attacks are becoming commonplace in the sector.

Last year the UK's colleges alone suffered 13 Ransomware attacks; by April this year, that number was 20. The NCSC wrote the aforementioned note to be inserted into college handbooks. Our research, shared with the AOC, showed exactly where the colleges were insecure and Not Secure, along with the technology partners providing services to the entire education sector. Pulling teeth with an old pair of pliers would be far easier than trying to assist, and the reason is they are being paid not to address and not to provide security. For anyone who actually is a security professional, such antics should go against the grain; however, their paymasters have a different outcome in play...

CASE EXCERPT 1—LIST OF US SCHOOLS AND COLLEGES VICTIM TO CYBERATTACKS IN 2020

Following is a list of US schools and colleges that were victims of cyberattacks in 2020. From 2016 to 2019, there were 855 cyberattacks on US school districts, nearly one a day, every day... The US government are allocating $millions for computer systems to support distant learning, which has been further highlighted during COVID-19. US Representative Josh Harder introduced a bill in Congress called the Protecting Students from Cybercrime Act. The bill's goal is to provide $25 million to schools to implement cyber security.

This weekend, St Petersburg High suffered a cyberattack by one of its own students that crashed 145 Pinella schools. When we researched the main website this morning, it was unsurprisingly rated at an F and scored a 0. This morning, I also wrote to Josh Harder, as unless the Education sector takes Internet security seriously, it will be more $millions wasted. For some unbelievable reason, most people still do not realise that the Internet and Security are not natural bedfellows. Much like going to the gym once will not make you fit for life, so if you set up a website and leave it, security will continually dwindle and became a major liability.

One can track Internet security cycles and pinpoint exactly at what point organisations are at their most vulnerable and exploitable. Again, it is still mind blowing that this fact is being overlooked and, worse, continually ignored.

Schools who were victims of cyberattacks and breached during 2020:

- Allegheny County Schools (NC) Ransomware attack
- Athens Independent School District (Texas) Ransomware attack

- Burke County Public Schools (NC) Ransomware attack
- Baugo Community Schools (Indiana) cyberattack
- Conejo Valley Unified school district (California) DDoS
- Cherry Hill School District Philadelphia Malware attack
- Gadsden Independent School District (Sunland Park NM) Ransomware attack
- Hartford Public Schools Ransomware attack
- Hamden school district (Connecticut) Malware attack
- Haywood County Schools Ransomware attack
- Humble Independent School District (Texas) DDoS attack
- Huntington Beach Unified High School District (California) Ransomware attack
- Jackson Public School District (Mississippi) Malware attack
- Jay Public School District (Oklahoma) virus
- King George County Schools Ransomware attack
- Lumberton Township Public Schools in Burlington County (New Jersey) Zoom malicious pornographic intrusion
- Miami-Dade Public Schools System cyberattack
- Mitchell County Schools (North Carolina) Ransomware attack
- The Mountain View-Los Altos High School District (California) Ransomware attack
- Community School Corporation of New Palestine Indiana (DDoS) cyberattack
- Penncrest School District (Pennsylvania) Ransomware attack (paid $10,000)
- Pittsburgh Unified School District of Pennsylvania Ransomware attack
- Ponca City Public Schools (Oklahoma) Ransomware attack
- Richmond school district (Michigan) Ransomware attack

- Surry County Schools Ransomware attack
- South Adams Schools (Indiana) Ransomware attack
- Southern Hancock School District (Indiana) DDoS attack
- St. Landry Parish schools (Louisiana) Malware attack
- Toledo Public School district (Ohio) cyberattack
- Ventura Unified school district (California) DDoS

Colleges attacked during 2020:

- Capital University Law School in (Columbus, Ohio)
- Columbia College Chicago Ransomware attack
- Michigan State University Ransomware attack
- New Mexico State University and the school's foundation virus
- Regis University (Denver Colorado) Ransomware attack, paid ransom
- University of California at San Francisco School of Medicine Ransomware attack, paid 1.14 million
- University of New Mexico School of Law (Albuquerque, NM)
- Wallace State Community College (Alabama) virus

We have recently embarked upon a program with the Department of Education here in the United Kingdom, and sadly the same lacking security is prevalent. Thirteen colleges were victims of Ransomware last year; that number had already been surpassed by the end of April this year. In the United Kingdom, we have League tables for schools, colleges, universities, and so on. They take numerous metrics to compile, including exam results. There is a strong argument to suggest a Cyber Rating League should be available, as cyberattacks, as we know, are not reducing—quite the opposite—and yet the education sector, as well as all sectors, sadly, is ignoring their critical Internet security. This situation is largely avoidable and simply must be invested in to ensure it is minimised.

21

THE WORLD'S LARGEST GLOBAL ECONOMIC SHIFT

Cyberattacks, including Ransomware, have been said by many leading Industry experts and leaders to be the world's most concerning issue that will cause companies to fail, economies to collapse, and ultimately the loss of lives. However, it is one thing to paint a scene from a future apocalyptic film and footage; but what exactly is being done to change it? Sadly, next to nothing, and waving the digital equivalent of the nuclear 'Fat Man' has deterred no one, as Paul Nakasone has said on more than one occasion.

Let us briefly look at the history of Ransomware since its early days and, in comparison, the affordable inconvenience that it causes. It is widely accepted that Ransomware commenced affecting companies in the mid 2000s.

In 2007, the FBI's Internet Complaint Centre received 1,783 Ransomware complaints that, when tallied up, had paid out a declared amount of $2.3 million. Last year, that number had increased to over 150 million complaints. Imagine if all these were factual Ransomware attacks, that is, hundreds of thousands of attacks a day…

The first documented Ransomware attack dates to 1989; they have exponentially grown ever since, and there is a direct correlation between website numbers, insecure domains, and Ransomware attacks. This is no coincidence. Ransomware, as we know, is a type of malicious software that, once it has gained access, looks to corrupt files and systems, blocking user access. The plain text data is exfiltrated, often unencrypted and then held hostage in exchange for payment, (ransom). Cyber criminals use encryption to ensure the data owners can no longer use the data, and without backups and copies of the data, the company is pretty much forced to settle a ransom payment or lose the data. Compounding that further, the company has, by default or design, been negligent to secure that data and will in

DOI: 10.1201/9781003278214-21

most cases be guilty of failing local Privacy Laws such as GDPR or the equivalent.

The key part that most companies, including major tech firms and far too many cyber security firms such as SolarWinds, are remiss in is the first element of any Ransomware attack, and that is to GAIN ACCESS. If a cybercriminal cannot gain access, they are unable to launch an attack. This part always amazes us, as part of any and every cybercriminal's reconnaissance is to identify companies, organisations, and even governments that are exposed and vulnerable. The only other criterion is whether the company is big enough and able to pay a ransom. So, the first place a cybercriminal looks is online and the websites of companies. It does not matter where they are, what they do, how many people work there, or the history of the company. The bigger they are the better, the more the ransom goes up. A cyber criminal's strategy and sequence of events will follow this or a similar pattern:

1 Identify insecure websites and domains using OSINT tech.
2 Once insecure websites are identified, gain insight into why they are insecure.
3 Plan suitable tactics and use various methods to exploit the vulnerabilities and gain access.
4 Successfully infiltrate the organisation and exfiltrate data, ideally plaintext data.
5 Encrypt plaintext data and alert the company of the exfiltrated, now encrypted, data.
6 Demand the Ransom, Rinse and repeat…

This method is repeated around 200,000 times a day, and many are successful at infiltrating organisations due to the fact No 1 in the list is a situation that is systemically available across all sectors and is an underlying, major contributing factor to the exponential increase in attacks. When we as a company find a charity, a SolarWinds, major insurance firm, government, or any other company and alert them to their vulnerabilities and insecure positions at the Internet, it is neither subjective nor a personal belief; it is a fact. When cyber criminals find the same situation, they will simply move to No 2 on the list. The clock is then ticking, and sadly, far too many egotistical so-called experts want to debate, argue, or defend their position instead of taking the

Actionable Intelligence and actually acting on it to secure their position. Put it this way: if a cybercriminal discovers a vulnerability, the same vulnerability we discover, and they find it at the same time, we are already far too late. They will exploit that vulnerability before we even know whom to try to contact. Often when we do find the right people, like the Bank of England, Lloyd's of London, the FCA, and hundreds of others, they want to throw it around for a few weeks, say they are aligned with the NCSC, who do nothing, and then ask if it could be reported on a separate website that allows a 'whistleblowing' or disclosure opportunity. We have not spent long enough trying to save their backsides and prevent a breach, and they are too busy to look at it. Equally, correct me if I am wrong, whistleblowing is a certainly a worthy consideration; however, it is more aligned to and supports internal staff more than an external consulting party that is not contracted to, working with, or partner of the company. It certainly is the way I see a whistle-blower. I commend the action, though I do not particularly like the term as it implies telling tales when executives have been negligent and on occasions even corrupt.

It is very easy to have a love-hate relationship with the NCSC, as those that know the often-questionable methods and alternative uses that the agencies have undertaken over the last two decades, the bundles of cash (now bitcoin) paid for Zero Day Exploits lately in a vain attempt to try to gain the upper hand in the cyberwar that they and the NSA created. I totally disagree with their tactics and the fact they actively suppress real security opportunities for fear of uncovering their prior antics and their concerns meaning their easy access might be reduced if the world finally realised and knew exactly what they are doing and have done. At least in traditional warfare, armies had the decency to wear a uniform to identify themselves. Equally, we are happy to call incompetence and negligence out, and sadly, the government have not been a credit to themselves time after time, be it the twenty-five-year Post Office debacle or the declaration that 120 countries and governments were being listened to illegally by the US government as they owned Crypto AG and Omnisec, the world's largest Cryptography and Encryption Original Equipment Manufacturers that came complete with CIA backdoors. The 120 governments included US allies. It is abundantly clear that the methods, tactics, and technology that the agencies used to gain mass data capture and harvesting became the MO for cybercriminals to emulate and create carbon copies for their nefarious activities. It would not be the first-time governments have facilitated illegal activities for their own gains.

It is also one of the world's worst-kept secrets that one of the first-ever investors in Facebook were the CIA, as they clearly saw the benefits of social media for future mass profiling and data capture. You'll all have seen the Jason Bourne film where the Director (played by Tommy Lee Curtis) tells the social media CEO that he was happy to take the government money to plant the backdoors. In fact, one could look at most major innovations that roll out, and invariably there will be a government involvement or warfare behind it; stop and think about that for just a minute. Airplanes, ships, firearms, automobiles, mass production of pretty much everything. The 3.8 litre engine of the magnificent Lightweight E Type Jaguar I raced so successfully throughout the late 2000s had its roots in military development from the 1950s.

Back to the history of Ransomware: privacy laws such as UKDPA and the European legislation have come into effect in the last several years to enforce better security and protection for the public's data. Additionally, specific laws and regulations such as HIPAA or the PCI Data Security Standard were created to provide guidelines for companies and organisations handling certain types of sensitive consumer information. These regulations provide a framework for the required safeguards, storage, and use practices for handling sensitive information, but these rules do not exist in all industries, nor do they definitively stop data breaches from occurring, as they are often advisory and not enforceable, although when companies are breached, they are often subject to fines from the various bodies. If they are found guilty and negligent of not maintaining the data securely and PII data has been exfiltrated, chances are Class Action Lawsuits will follow, and when this occurs, it is typically a group that is brought together to take group action. Recent breaches that were followed by fines and then Class Action Lawsuits include Marriott, Equifax, BA, and easyJet. easyJet had 9 million people's PII data, and £2000 per claimant is being sought. If every one of the 9 million claimants were successful, that would cost easyJet £18 billion in Class Action Lawsuits plus costs. Cyberattacks and Ransomware are no longer minor irritants; they can and do topple many companies, no matter what their size. Although the SolarWinds breach was not motivated by Ransomware, it will end up costing Solar-Winds and their clients many tens, if not hundreds of $billions to reme-diate from the Sunburst malicious attacks that, like the Marriott and Equifax breaches, let alone the first digital weapon, Stuxnet, all used, or was due to a lack of PKI controls and compromised digital certificates to cause and facilitate their attacks or service outages.

Ransomware has been around pretty much since the advent of com-puting; however, it has greatly increased and advanced in many ways over the last fifteen to twenty years. One thing for sure is the methods listed previously vary little inasmuch that access must be gained as in numbers 1 to 6 on the list previously shared. The only difference may be the automation and Advanced Persistent Threats that constantly catch companies out that are insecure by default, or design. Throw in cloud computing, insecure DNS, and the CDNs often required to enable acceptable latency and geographical distribution, and it can add fur-ther complexities and vulnerabilities, as our research continually shows. Throw in Certificate Authorities, most of whom have been breached in the last few years, and DNSs, who have also been breached, and it is all too easy to see the minefield of connectivity across the globe. Let's Encrypt had to recall 3 million digital certificates only a year ago due to incorrect issuance, and Digicert blamed their first breach upon a supplying vendor. They have yet to lay blame for the second breach; however, when we wrote to them a year ago, we did inform them that their CDN had all 65,535 ports open. The same CDN was manag-ing a CNI that we had researched and found three RATs on a single server. A RAT is a Remote Access Trojan, and I suspect the term is carried over from the Cold War; however, a digital RAT can sit on a server and capture data via backdoors. Yes, you guessed it, RATs were perfected and used extensively by governments as part of their over-all digital dominance. Many companies and tech giants succumbed to the 'encouragement' of such RATs for commercial favour and benefit, and many denied their activity for decades; however, as with all digital eavesdropping techniques, these myths soon become known and then used against everyone. As General Michael Hayden said, once a back-door is in place, it can become a backdoor for others. It certainly has been and continues to be.

Ransomware attacks have become a massive business and cause major inconvenience, costs, and potentially threaten lives, such as when healthcare attacks, which have become widespread lately, are deployed. We empathise with each company that becomes a victim of a Ransomware attack and wish the governments would take such attacks and disruptions more seriously. Executive Orders and throwing $billions at friends and family cyber security companies that are not themselves secure and expecting a different outcome is nothing short of insanity. What is urgently and critically required is to acknowledge the access that is being used and manipulated, that is, the Internet connections, and then to address them. Our suggestion is to say, like drivers on our roads, if you are unsafe or insecure and threaten other motorists, you will not be allowed on the roads. The Internet is our digital highway and requires much better controls. Is it so farfetched that a company like SolarWinds, for example, needs to be protected from itself and if the search engine companies, instead of saying Not Secure on the address bar, just stopped all search capability and access, surely that would protect SolarWinds and all their clients? We would certainly see a behavioural change, as the Internet is seen by many as the lifeblood of their businesses, and they would certainly focus on their security if it meant they could no longer trade or have a digital presence; something to think about for sure.

In the first half of 2020, some 8 billion people's PII data was compromised, the equivalent of every human on the planet. Add digital identity theft, illegal personal loans, debts, and even worse, organised crime making claims for years due to data theft, and you can count the $billions and $billions. There is a saying in show business: 'You ain't seen nothing yet', and my fear is we are entering that phase in the cyberworld. Cybercriminals act like farmers and take what the crop they can yield and nurture it, and then come back for the next harvest to make sure it is sustainable; the challenge is we are not securing it with a similar defensive strategy. Our research across multiple sectors, governments, education, military, healthcare, and others demonstrates a systemic lack of basic security. There is a reason the NCSC have a B+ Rating and 80 score but are content for, say, Mersey Rail, easyJet, or Travelex to maintain an F Rating and 0 score (all breached). The question this chapter leaves the reader with is this: Why do the NSA, NCSC, GCHQ, and US and UK governments not enforce a regime of security connected to the Internet? If anyone has a different answer to the one we have, please do not hesitate to email me.

22

It Is Not Setting Goals Too High, but Setting Them Too Low and Achieving Them

We constantly hear the statement that everyone should be prepared to have their data compromised, stolen, and abused, and that is from our own governments. The title of this chapter is very apt. It is also a sad fact that our own governments have gladly abused the position to infiltrate organisations and other governments due to their targets lack of knowledge and ability to ensure Internet-secure positions. It is also questionable as to why, even though it is a conflict of interest, the US, UK, and other governments have not educated the masses in Internet security, they are finally and we have been told by many, the sharing of information has all the hallmarks, and fingerprints of our efforts and work.

Over the last weekend, we decided to research some of the biggest names in the industry to see exactly how seriously they take Internet security and that of their clients. The two primary organisations are the Centre of Internet Security, cisecurity.org, and the Information Systems Audit and Control Association.

On the website of cisecurity.org, it states:

The Centre for Internet Security, Inc. (CIS®) makes the connected world a safer place for people, businesses, and governments through our core competencies of collaboration and innovation.

We are a community-driven nonprofit, responsible for the CIS Controls® and CIS Benchmarks™, globally recognized best practices for securing IT systems and data. We lead a global community of IT professionals to continuously evolve these standards and provide products and services to proactively safeguard against emerging threats. Our CIS

Hardened Images® provide secure, on-demand, scalable computing environments in the cloud.

CIS is home to the Multi-State Information Sharing and Analysis Centre® (MS-ISAC®), the trusted resource for cyber threat prevention, protection, response, and recovery for U.S. State, Local, Tribal, and Territorial government entities, and the Elections Infrastructure Information Sharing and Analysis Centre® (EI-ISAC®), which supports the rapidly changing cybersecurity needs of U.S. elections offices.

CIS state that their vision is to lead the global community to secure our ever-changing connected world and that their mission:

> is to make the connected world a safer place by developing, validating, and promoting timely best practice solutions that help people, businesses, and governments protect themselves against pervasive cyber threats.

It is very encouraging and comforting to read, and indeed believe, there is this major body, supported by US governments and major corporations, advising and leading best practices within the often confusing and insecure world that is the Internet. Given their position, status, and gravitas, one would naturally assume, without being too assumptive, that cisecurity.org would undoubtedly be securely connected to the Internet. Sadly, and rather embarrassingly they are not. We researched and wrote to CIS yesterday and sent a copy to the CISA confirming CIS had a security Rating of F and a score of 0. In other words, their Rating and score could not be worse. The Rating for CIS in June 2016 was healthy B and 70; then that September, it slipped to a D and 30, and then finally in August 2020, it went all the way down to a Rating of F and a score of 0. This Rating and score are a direct result of lacking HSTS headers, redirection issues, third-party content, insecure coding issues, and X-Content and XSS issues. To reconfirm, the Rating of F and score of 0 are the worst possible Rating and score for Internet security, and this is the Centre for Internet Security, depended upon by thousands of organisations and governments, no doubt with a vast amount of client data.

We wrote to the CIS Chief Technology Officer and provide screenshots of our research and findings and are awaiting a response.

We then looked at ISACA. ISACA stands for Information Systems Audit and Control Administration. On their website, it states the following:

ISACA started in 1967 by a small group of individuals with similar jobs auditing controls in computer systems that were becoming more critical to their organizations' operations. This group saw the need for a centralized source of information and guidance in the field and formalized in 1969, incorporating as the EDP Auditors Association. In 1976 the association formed an education foundation to undertake large-scale research efforts to expand the knowledge and value of the IT governance and control field. Previously known as the Information Systems Audit and Control Association®, ISACA now goes only by its acronym to reflect the broad range of IT governance professionals we serve.

Today, ISACA's constituency of more than 165,000 strong worldwide is characterized by its diversity. These professionals live and work in more than 180 countries and cover a variety of professional IT-related positions in the disciplines of IS/IT audit, risk, security, and governance as well as educators, consultants, and regulators. Some are new to their careers, others are at middle management levels, and still others are in the most senior ranks. They work in nearly all industry categories, including financial and banking, public accounting, government and the public sector, utilities, and manufacturing. This diversity enables members to learn from each other and exchange widely divergent viewpoints on a variety of professional topics.

Given ISACA's incredible position, relationships with regulators and the senior ranks within the world of technology, governance, audit, banks, FS, and thousands of others, one might assume that ISACA's own business, connected to the Internet would be compliant to privacy and security laws by being secure. Sadly, ISACA are also falling foul, maintaining an Internet security of F and score of 0. ISACA had that Rating on 19 May 2016 and look as if they have maintained it ever since. So, quite possibly, not only are they insecure now, but they may also well have been for the last five years. That would concern me greatly as a member of their executive team and board, speaking of which, back in November 2020, I connected with one of ISACA's board and sent a friendly, polite email. I received a simple one-line 'No thank you'. So, when our research on ISACA this weekend showed an awful F and 0, I shared the information with the same connected board member. I guessed the buck stopped somewhere, and surely a board member was aware of the onslaught of cyberattacks and quite possibly the critical importance of Internet security along with ISACA's reputation. I received a reply to the information and was told that she would pass it on. It was then that I received the following message: 'Well if you're trying to sell something to ISACA don't start with a board member'. It was at that point I responded, on a Bank Holiday Monday: 'Tracey, please feel free to totally ignore my effort to share a major concern with you. It is no skin off my nose, as I have alerted you as a professional reaching out to a contact. If ISACA choose to ignore, that is perfectly fine. Warmest regards, Andy'. This morning I have received a further email stating, 'Your marketing effort is hardly positive, Mr Jenkins'. I am unsure why this board member cannot get my name right (it is Jenkinson) or thinks I am on a marketing campaign. To put this into perspective, ISACA have the same woefully inadequate security Rating as every company we have researched post breach over the last two years, including SolarWinds, numerous states, Bose, Canada Post, the Canadian government, the Brazilian government, and hundreds and hundreds of others.

In 2015/2016, Special Agent Adrian Hawkins tried for over six months to notify the OPM (Office of Personnel Management) that they were being breached, and no one batted an eyelid; it was only after a meeting, 1.2 mile away from the FBI offices that Special Agent Hawkins worked at, that the infiltration was taken seriously. During this breach, it is accepted that every serviceman and woman's details had been exfiltrated, including all the PII data of current and previous security-cleared personnel and their families.

I was also contacted over the weekend by the Head of Strategy at CISA, like the CIA but add an S, like the way Google added an S in 2018 to HTTP(S) for security. I was asked if I could help them, 'attract the best people', to which I replied, I fear you do not want the best people; you just want people who dance to your tune. I received a reply stating the requirement was to: 'Maintain status while promoting an internal body to reinforce groupthink is the MO. I need people like you to get the word out and attract candidates who can change CISA for the good'.

I emailed several reports on our research across all 50 US states in the lead-up to the US Presidential election which showed a systemic failing of basic security at each state, Delaware being the worst, with another report on education and a final one on healthcare.

I cited the issues of organisations being breached whilst maintaining sub optimal positions and maintaining that insecure position after paying a ransom. Clemson University were awarded $111 million to teach the manufacturing sector in the United States about cybercrime prevention, during which time the University's homepage was Not Secure due to invalid SSL certificates. What Clemson were going to teach only goodness knows; certainly not basic Internet security, that's for sure.

When government organisations like the CNSS allow domains to become Not Secure due to obsolete SSL certificates, with all that implies for security, and when the MPDC; CNA, the Insurance Giant; then AXA get breached and all are running F- and 0-rated Internet security, someone, somewhere needs to wake up and realise this is a fundamental issue, and that issue is Internet security, or the lack thereof.

We have spelled this out so many times and will continue to do so: criminals need to gain digital access to your enterprise, your network. If they cannot, they cannot attack you; that is a basic premise. Think of it like American football, you cannot score a Touchdown if you do not have possession. Cybercriminals equally cannot launch attacks unless they have access.

By connecting to the Internet, you have much to gain; connect insecurely, however, and you have everything to lose.

Finally, in response to the Head of Strategy at CISA, I confirmed: give us the autonomy and support we need, and we will drive the change required to stop the self-inflicted siege of cyberattacks the world is currently suffering, or we will die trying. I do hope the last point was not taken literally...

CASE STUDY 2—MIND THE GAP

It is June 4, and all US national press is covering the latest revelations of cyberattacks on transportation systems in New York and Massachusetts, heightening concerns about the threat to U.S. businesses and essential services Wednesday, after hackers held hostage the world's largest meat processor (JBS Foods) earlier this week to ransom. However, research on each one of the organisations making headlines this week, for all the wrong reasons, shows each one, as always, has woefully inadequate sub optimal Internet-connected security. So why is nobody listening or taking action, even after being provided actionable intelligence? The press, along with the government, are continually laying blame on Russia and China, however, organisations are at fault due to continually and systemically failing to keep their own house in order, in this case, basic security. Think of it like this: if you owned a magnificent 1962 Drophead E Type Jaguar and parked it in full view in a high-crime area, keys in the ignition, and then left it for a day, much less 365 days, would you expect it to be there the next day? I rest my case, and yet SolarWinds, Colonial, JBS foods, MTA, and thousands of other organisations are doing this every day, not with a Drophead E Type but their organisations, it is not even difficult as it is made so simple.

Some six months earlier in November 2020, I personally wrote to the mayor's office in NYC to inform, then alert, them of the findings from our research in NYC and the plethora of NYC's sub optimal websites. We are not talking a minor issue here or there; we are talking about fully exposed, vulnerable, and highly exploitable Internet-connected domains that could, if discovered and targeted, bring NYC to a grinding halt. This is no movie set; this was reality. We are prepared for the worst but hope for the best. Little did we know that six months later, MTA would indeed be the victim of a cyberattack. We received, some eight weeks later, on 8 January, the following email from Ben, NYC's deputy Cyber Security Officer.

> Andy,
>
> Thank you for reaching out to the Office of the Mayor regarding the security of the City of New York's web presence. Your correspondence was recently forwarded to the Department of Information Technology and Telecommunications (DoITT) for a response, so, first, let me apologize for the delay in the City's reply to your message.

Of course, DoITT's Information Security team shares your concerns for the security of NYC's web presence, and we appreciate your feedback. If you have discovered a specific vulnerability in our environment, we would greatly appreciate it if you could provide specific details so that we can adequately remediate them. Rest assured that any findings you identify will be brought to the attention of my management, and we will make every effort to properly address them.

Once again, I thank you for your concern and for taking the time to bring this important matter to the Mayor's attention.

I look forward to hearing back from you.

Regards,

Ben

Ben Fernandes, CISSP, CISM, CISA, CRISC, CGEIT
Deputy Chief Information Security Officer
    NYC Department of Information Technology & Telecommunications

I know we are all busy; however, given the position Ben holds, the evidence we supplied, and the fact we had assisted the FBI in 2020 before the Presidential elections and discovered a Korean DNS within the central voting system, one might like to think a slightly speedier response might be pertinent. I guess he did apologise for the delay in responding; the fact the United States had associated costs and losses in the tens of $billions to cybercrime during that same period seems to be of little concern. I am incredibly busy 14–16 hours a day, every day, and I replied to Ben on the same day, within minutes. My reply included further information as well as examples of similar transport operators, namely STM and SEPTA, who had both been victims of cyberattacks, one in the United States and one in Canada. Both SEPTA and STM had the same sub optimal domain positions, both pre and post breaches, as many of those NYC official websites, including MTA. I also added the fact we had recently shared similar information with Ritchie Torres's office, as he had been incredibly vocal campaigning for a central NY Cyber Centre and had himself, by virtue of maintaining a sub optimal and insecure website, flouting privacy laws, and making the organisation a target for cyber criminals. It is a sad situation that government offices and corporations will do so much more to accept being victims of Ransomware; negotiate with cyber criminals; and make payment, often in $millions, than listen to logic and consider evidence even when provided free of charge. Furthermore, it is bordering on sheer arrogance and rudeness for organisations such as MTA, NYC, and Ritchie Torres to take the actionable intelligence and either take no action, as in the case of Ritchie Torres, just ignore, as well as NYC and MTA, without any gratitude, acknowledgement, or further communication...

Dear Ben

I hope you are well, and can I just say that although I am not an out and out political person, I am very sorry to see the absolute nonsense the US is currently going through.

Interestingly, this week the NSA have followed our lead and taken our research and findings onboard to release their information on obsolete TLS protocol configuration, we are very flattered.

So, one of the domains that we would like to highlight is www.bt.mta.info that is running a Not Secure domain and has done for several months. Also, interesting domain hijacking, made possible due to insecure domains, was the initial infiltration point of Decembers catastrophic SolarWinds breach, in other words the same as the domain we are informing you of.

We would urge a full research and audit of all NYC domains and would be delighted to assist.

Regards,
Andy
PS the attachment of Septa and STM is attached and who were both breached in 2020 and both had Not Secure domains.

Several weeks passed, and almost out of the blue, a security team member from MTA contacted me to ask if I could share the security 'gaps' they had missed and would I be OK to take a call. Several people were copied in the email, and to suit their team, the call was set up for 12 February at 22:00 UK time. I believe twelve, possibly as many as fourteen, people from the IT and Security team from MTA were on the call. We discussed our research and shared information with them on several of the MTA domains that were using obsolete SSL certificates, were misconfigured, or were using mismatched certificates which rendered the website Not Secure, exposed, and highly vulnerable. The situation unequivocally made MTA exposed, vulnerable, and easily exploitable. A lady called Valerie played the lead role to a great extent from the MTA side and requested further information in an email the following day. I duly obliged and forwarded further information on the same day. MTA then went silent. I followed up via email on 16 February and then 23 February. Not a word, not even confirmation of the intelligence shared, a big fat zero. Until confirmation this week of a cyberattack, several months after I started alerting them to their insecure and highly vulnerable position, which they chose to ignore. Our research post breach today, 5 June, shows nowmta.info is running an F Rating for Internet security several weeks post their breach. I emailed Ben and Valerie separately to share my displeasure with the sequence of events and the fact MTA are still insecure; you guessed it, nothing...

This week's coverage by literally every US major paper is the typical, pumped-up chests being pounded and blaming Russia, China, and anyone and everyone else for these so-called 'sophisticated' attacks. It is a futile, useless blame game being played out before your very eyes. Today I have just written the following open letter to Ms Anne Neuberger, the Deputy National Security Advisor for Cyber and Emerging Technology, on LinkedIn for 600 million people to see:

Dear Ms Neuberger

I read with interest your memo this week alerting Corporate America of the threats and dangers of cyberattacks and ransomware.

I understand this is an emotive subject and also understand that far too many people, particularly governments and agencies, may be reluctant to accept the glaringly obvious, however every breach at the government, SolarWinds, Colonial, CNA, JBS Foods and MTA, and thousands more, are guilty, and should therefore be held responsible, for their basic security negligence. This systemic problem is nowhere more so than where they are connected to the Internet. Most are still woefully insecure, which is simply shocking.

We have shared findings with CISA and Paul Nakasone recently and continue to offer our assistance.

In conclusion, to best prevent such attacks, corporate America must stop making itself an easy, exploitable target.

Best regards
Andy

Ms Neuberger has stated

Companies should implement multifactor authentication, bolster security teams, regularly test backups and update patches, test incident response plans and separate and limiting Internet access to operational networks. "The threats are serious, and they are increasing. We urge you to take these critical steps to protect your organizations and the American public,"

Sadly, Ms Neuberger stopped short of alerting the American public that they must ensure their Internet-connect domains have basic security that was fit for purpose, as the Internet-connected domains acted as the very doorways that provided access for infiltration and Ransomware attacks. These attacks are NOT sophisticated; they are opportunistic and prey on the oversight, ignorance, and even incompetence of those charged with security. Even when we 'gifted' the information and concerns to the NYC Mayor's office, Department for Transport, and MTA, they did nothing and then a while later became victims to a cyberattack. US legislators and legal professionals need to hold those responsible to account; sadly, far too much playing the victim card and calling the cyber insurance provider playing the victim is being accepted. Nothing will change until a planet-scale change of attitude takes place.

In addition, this week, the Steamship Authority became the latest victims to suffer an attack. On their website, they were taking their communication capability seriously by notifying the public of the sequence of events. However, their communication capability is clearly far greater than their security ability, as, like many before them, they have limited to no clue why they were victims of a cyberattack. A quick look at their address bar yesterday showed there, bold as brass, they are telling the world they are a travel company and know nothing at all about Internet security, and there it is, confirming the fact, a Not Secure text. In the security world, this is basic security at its lowest. It not only makes them a target, but it is a near guarantee they will be infiltrated, disrupted, and hit with a ransom demand. Just like the recent cyber assault in Florida of 145 schools being shut down by a seventeen-year-old pupil, almost by mistake, these attacks will keep coming thick and fast, and most certainly do not need state backing. All these organisations and schools are maintaining F-Rated security for their domains and are open to being easily identified and exploited. It is a Ransomware and cyber criminals' sweet shop: fill your bags, as nobody is bothering to look; but, my goodness, everyone is happy to blame everyone else for their own negligence and incompetence.

Corporate America is like a sitting duck and will continue to be so until Internet security is 1) acknowledged and 2) prioritised. We have previously greatly assisted MITRE CWE, NCSC, FBI, CISA, and many, many more. Internet security must be fit for purpose and become mainstream, or corporate America and the rest of the world will continue to burn.

Late this week, we received confirmation that Scripps Health-care had announced that they paid a Ransomware payment. Quick research confirmed Scripps were, and still are, maintaining a sub optimal Internet security position. Their F and 0 Ratings are as bad as security registers. The F can stand for FAIL; it can also stand for something else. If you are maintaining, storing, sharing, or receiving PII data and need to keep that data secure, chances are, if you maintain an F, you more than likely will be f... ed.

It gives us no pleasure to see an organisation like MTA become a victim of a cyberattack. Saying 'we did warn' you helps nobody, however, we did, six months ago. ... MIND THE GAP.

23

AVOIDING THE APOCALYPSE

This year we have witnessed the aftermath of the SolarWinds cyberattack, Colonial Pipeline, New Zealand Central Bank, water treatment CNI attacks, and police departments, among hundreds and thousands of other cyberattacks, and now the world's largest meat producer: on 30 May, JBS Foods was subject to a cyberattack, rendering many of their abattoirs unable to work as normal and causing rumours of thousands of staff being stood down. Although it is too early to say and no demands have yet been made, most cyberattacks fall into one of two categories, IP theft and disruption or Ransomware. The latter is more than likely the case for this global, $billion organisation but is yet to be confirmed.

What is sure, just like the run-on fuel because of the recent Colonial Pipeline cyberattack, meat is already experiencing a high demand, and prices are starting to rapidly increase in certain markets. The attack, first noted and reported on 30 May, two days ago, is said to be affecting the servers supporting the North American and Australian IT systems. All affected systems were immediately suspended, and various outlets and authorities affected were notified. According to JBS, backup servers were not affected; however, I would be very surprised if that were the case, as connectivity is the key here, as is the fact that the servers were initially infiltrated in the first place sounds highly likely.

Literally, due to JBS, like all other organisations in this, and other sectors, they are heavily reliant upon digital capability and Internet connectivity for record keeping, regulatory documentation, sorting, and numerous other critical functions. Unfortunately, as we witnessed in the recent Colonial Pipeline cyberattack, it is not the fact they could not continue pumping gas down the fuel lines; Colonial halted pumping the gas because the systems created an allocation and invoicing challenge. The reported ransom of $4.4 million will pale into insignificance compared to overall costs of the disruption caused,

DOI: 10.1201/9781003278214-23

and sadly, as Colonial remain F and 0 rated for their Internet security, as well as now knowing what, at the PKI level, has gone on or been planted during the infiltration, I would suggest Colonial, along with many, many other companies caught napping and continuing to be negligent of their own security, will be breached on more than one occasion, possibly several. Until they finally take the required action to address and remediate their insecure position, nothing will change.

JBS Foods face an immediate halt at many of their facilities and thousands of chilled carcasses from the cattle slaughtered the day before the attack. It is not the physical task of boning the carcasses; it is the record keeping which will now have to be manual. It is believed that the slower, manual process will affect shipping documentation, labelling, inventorying, and records without computer systems. As such, the resultant boxed meat is more than likely to serve the local market. Coles, the supermarket giant that is supplied extensively by JBS Foods, has already looked at other suppliers. The knock-on effects from such a cyberattack will be incredibly difficult to calculate.

Within minutes, literally, of hearing of the JBS Foods Cyberattack, our research went on the hunt for vulnerabilities. It was not long before we found several JBS Foods homepages rated with F and 0 ratings. The website, connected to all international domains, would and easily could have been used to laterally move around other parts of the network just as SolarWinds and Colonial suffered, and it is no coincidence that both SolarWinds and Colonial had, and still have, Internet security Ratings of F and 0. Now either incompetence and negligence are of monumental, biblical proportions or being facilitated. As I constantly ask the question, complacent or complicit? We know, as should everyone, most certainly in security or IT, the Internet was weaponised many years ago; it allows all computing functions around the world, and it can act like a two-way valve unless you control and manage the one-way valve that is called security. Information and data should not be available to anyone wanting to look or be taken by anyone willing to break the law and exfiltrate it.

Senator Mike Rounds said on 25 May, just five days earlier, that there were major issues with beef packers controlling prices. He said, 'Consumers are paying way too much for beef at the grocery store. Meanwhile, our independent cattle producers—who we rely on to feed the world—are going broke'. Between the consumer and the producer sit four large beef packing companies that control over 80% of the processing market. These four packers seemingly can control prices at their will, and thus have realised significant profits, while both the US beef consumers and independent cattle producers pay the price. Mike Rounds went on to say; 'The time has come to fix this. We are launching a bipartisan, nationwide effort to defend our consumers and cattlemen. We have announced that we will be sending a letter to the Department of Justice asking them to examine whether the control the meatpackers have of the beef processing market violates US antitrust laws. We are asking members of Congress—House Senate, Republican and Democrat—to support this effort'. Within a week JBS Foods suffered a cyberattack. I am sure it is just a coincidence; however, many do not believe in such things.

The institution that is McDonalds may be adversely affected should the situation not be remediated quickly, and a long time veteran red meat processor told Beef Central that prices were expected to see a slight rise depending upon the duration of JBS's outage. He also said 'Nobody could have foreseen this coming, but it represents a problem of incredible proportions for the company'. To be candid, the red meat processors, along with the JBS Foods Executive team, are not in the field of IT security, or it would have been very easy to foresee this event and many more occurring. There is a major consideration for shorting a company, an organisation that remains insecure, as that price will certainly be affected if and when they suffer a cyberattack. Look at the last chapter: when a company has a general erosion of their security position connected to the Internet, immaterial of whether it was by design or default (complacent or complicit), that company is going to be infiltrated, and all our research shows that it will be when the company has declining and insecure Internet security. This is an interesting theory and one that we have tested hundreds of times. One must only consider supply and demand, prices, and behaviour during the weeklong Colonial cyberattack to realise the repercussions of such events.

No matter what company you are with or what sector you work in, car manufacturing, accounting, legal, banking, insurance, Critical National Infrastructure, water, food, energy, or a plethora of others, like it or not, you are also effectively a technology company. That has implications from years ago: sending a fax that became an email, and so on. All companies, literally every company you can think of, is totally reliant upon computing for one thing or another. I remember many years ago when my office, an old Lloyd's Bank office with incredible cabling and Internet connectivity, went offline due to works in the adjoining road and cables being severed. They were so totally reliant on their screens and computers that over ten of the staff started making coffee and declared they were simply unable to work because of the outage. This is the position innovation and progress has created, and we have become more and more dependent upon technology and the Internet. As companies like Colonial and JBS Foods, certainly not out and out technology companies and will never think of themselves as such, come to a grinding halt because of a cyberattack, a cyberattack that preyed on their inability to act like a technology company with all that entails, especially so far as lax security measures are concerned. In truth, I am furious at the agencies and governments for happily leaving the general public to try playing catch up all the while manipulating their ignorance for their own purposes and data harvesting. The original framework, tools, and methods for cybercrime were invented by our governments over the last 20 years, and it is being used en masse against the entire world, and yet they still happily ignore the facts, as they do not want to be called out. The reality is cybercrime in the main is the single largest own goal ever, and nobody is brave enough to stand and be counted, apart from us that is.

From the early days of Stuxnet, initially under President Bush and then President Obama, who, let us not forget, had Biden by his side, all witnessed and sanctioned cyberwar without any thought or consideration of the repercussions. From the early days after the 9/11 attacks in the United States, the US more than ever wanted to call on a fight and sadly paid very little attention to defence, HUGE MISTAKE. That situation is why the United States is considered by many the melting pot of the vast majority of cyberattacks. Time after time, company after company fall foul of totally insecure positions. Sure, they are ignorant and incompetent of ensuring they have robust and fit-for-purpose security, as they know no different. As we have discovered, even the thought leaders at MITRE CWE, CISE, CNSS, ISACA, RTF, and hundreds of others simply unable to lead by example and are themselves insecure, using obsolete, invalid certificates and misconfigured, mismatched, and easily exploited websites. The governments had a field day and infiltrated company after company, government after government without any consideration and, more likely as not, without higher permission or sanction. Nobody knew then, very few know now, and that has become the MO for all cyber-crimes; the headlights shining blinding the deer is the position we are all currently in. It was self-inflicted and possibly the world's largest ever mistake. It is not an easy one to fix; however, we have offered our services to the government if they want our help. I truly hope it is not too late.

Now imagine a few of these events occurring concurrently, and you are seeing a perfect storm. That is exactly the journey we are all on, and it is happening right before our eyes. Conspiracy theories of government and agency intervention aside for one moment, we are currently witnessing global systemic negligence that will disrupt every area of people's lives, and unless we address them head on, we are fast falling into a global pandemic of apocalyptic proportions that is unprecedented and will witness a great shift in economic strength and control within just a few years.

24

If a Clever Person Learns from Their Mistakes and a Wise Person Learns from the Mistakes of Others, What Is a Person Who Learns from Neither Known As?

On 15 May 2020, I emailed Thomas, an executive of ExaGrid, and shared a screenshot showing ExaGrid's Internet security Rating. I concluded with the line: 'Thomas, ExaGrid's Internet security needs checking as the attached indicates'. To which Thomas responded, 'Hi Andy, I am not sure I'm following, would you like to expand?' I went back to Thomas on the same day and said, 'Hi Thomas, as I say, I would suggest your security team check the Internet security connectivity as a Rating of F and 0 is the worst possible security Rating. If they are unable to discover these issues, let me know and we would be happy to engage and assist, regards, Andy'. I did not hear back from Thomas.

We have just learned that ExaGrid, quite likely unknown to Thomas, were targeted and became victims of a Ransomware attack by the Conti Gang, who claimed to have infiltrated ExaGrid's network for a period of a month. After negotiating, a figure of $2.6 million was paid in Bitcoin to the Conti Gang, who then released the decryption key.

ExaGrid' s homepage states: 'Fastest Backups, Fastest Recoveries. Industry's Best Ransomware Recovery. Unparalleled, Cost-effective Scale-out'. What it does not state is: We are wide open to being infiltrated and attacked with Ransomware, as our Internet security Rating and score are F and 0...

DOI: 10.1201/9781003278214-24

The cyber criminals got straight to the point, and said: 'As you already know, we infiltrated your network and stayed in it for more than a month (enough to study all of your documentation), encrypted your file servers and SQL servers, and downloaded all important information with a total weight of more than 800 GB'.

The negotiations commenced, and a figure was agreed on and paid, which then released the decryption key, and then ExaGrid lost it. Rather embarrassingly, ExaGrid had to go back to the cyber criminals and ask for a second decryption key. You really could not make this stuff up. ExaGrid have an impressive client list, a list that one could consider highly sensitive due to their work with various agencies and governments: General Dynamics, Northrop Grumman, Accenture, Boeing, Cap Gemini, and so on. Interestingly, there are inevitably several that have been breached themselves by the same Internet security negligence, such as Bose recently. I am positive that all these critical, government suppliers should unequivocally be undertaking due diligence on their third-party supply chains and data storage providers such as ExaGrid; however, that simply has not been the case. What is clear here is that ExaGrid and all their clients and customers took limited to no due diligence and if the Conti Ransomware Gang were in their systems for a month, they could have gained access to pretty much whatever they wanted. It would not be too much to consider a spate of consequential hacks on ExaGrid's customers due to the data being retained. Such an attack could be like the recent Ransomware attack on CNA, the US Cyber Insurer, who also paid and have an ongoing Internet security Rating of F and 0. The criminals exfiltrated data on CNA's customers on levels of policy and Ransomware cover so they could launch attacks with the least resistance, knowing full well the Insurer would settle the claim. Besides, if CNA could be a victim of one of these so-called and awfully intrusive 'sophisticated' attacks, so could their clients. The fact is none of these attacks are ever sophisticated; they are opportunistic and prey on the weak, vulnerable, and ignorant. By neglecting the Internet connection and security of websites, their insecure position acts like a beacon for easy infiltration and exfiltration of plaintext data. They then can extract, encrypt, and sell back their encrypted data with a decryption key. For cyber criminals, it is a simple process such that they can eat, sleep, rinse, and repeat and leave a trail of devastation and losses. One thing I know for sure is if I were any of the clients of ExaGrid,

I would certainly be checking what was being stored and my own Internet domain connectivity. Remember, if you connect, it can be a two-way valve without proper controls or management. It will hardly come as a surprise that companies of this level are victims of attacks; however, how accommodating they are to enable such attacks is simply shocking.

Sometimes it may be a case of learning the hard way; however, as the saying goes, a clever person learns by their mistakes, a wise one by the mistakes of others. I guess a new saying we could add to this is only a complete fool learns from neither. An example of this is UHNJ (University Hospital of New Jersey) or the Freight Forward Air Corporation. In a statement, Jérôme Segura, director of threat intelligence at Malwarebytes, said

> The trucking and logistics industry is an attractive target because many of its customers are expecting deliveries, ransomware attacks have been around for years. They involve malware that infiltrates a system or systems and then encrypts data. The attackers then demand a sum of money, usually in the form of bitcoin to unlock the data.

UHNJ and Forward Air were at the time of their cyberattacks maintaining sub optimal Internet-connected websites; both had security Ratings and scores of F and 0. I guess both these companies fall into the category of only a complete fool learning from neither, as both were victims; both paid a ransom; and both, several months later, have learned absolutely nothing, as both are maintaining F and 0 security Ratings.

A possible makeup of cybercriminal and their activity can be as follows:

Phase 1—Information Gathering
Phase 2—Reconnaissance
Phase 3—Discovery and Scanning
Phase 4—Vulnerability Assessment
Phase 5—Gain Access
Phase 6—Maintain Access
Phase 7—Exfiltrate Data
Phase 8—Demand Ransom

It is imperative to understand that through Phases 1–4, cyber criminals, in the main, are identifying organisations that have poor Internet security at their websites, and a holy grail is a website that uses obsolete SSL certificates, rendering the site exposed, vulnerable, and exploitable. What is more, as we have previously mentioned, the domain can be subject to domain hijacking and takeover, and ultimately an assailant can take C2, as was the case with SolarWinds. As we now know, the SolarWinds breach is one of the world's largest single breaches, which consequentially affected some 18,000 customers, including the US government and US Treasury. What we also know is SolarWinds have, simply unbelievably, maintained their F and 0 Internet insecure connections, which again must fall into the category of only a fool learning from neither. Rather disturbingly and incredibly concerning is the fact that Colonial, SolarWinds, ExaGrid and numerous government departments and backed organisations such as the Ransomware Task Force, CNSS, the US Treasury, and a huge raft of others all are not maintaining secure positions, and all clearly lack strong controls or management of their Internet-connected domains. This fact alone is costing the world, most of all the United States, $trillions annually.

I read with interest yesterday that Microsoft are automating HTTPS to their Edge Browser for secure browsing. The release, part of their Microsoft 365 roadmap, was announced in April this year and should start being rolled out in July. It is certainly a step in the right direction. As you will recall, Google migrated from HTTP to HTTPS in 2018 after several years of pontification; however, that adoption was not unilateral. This action should make hundreds of thousands of websites more secure; however, my concern is that a tad like Cyber Insurance, it might encourage people to be lazy and continue ignoring their security, expecting it to be automated by others. Websites will still massively be more secure by having controlled and managed security such as HSTS, cookie policies, and third-party scripts. Yes, Man-in-The-Middle attacks could and should be reduced; however, a holistic approach to security must be adhered to, reinforced, and carried out with discipline and assurance if we are ever to see noteworthy reductions in cyber- and Ransomware attacks.

In a previous chapter, we touched on avoiding the apocalypse, and that term is not to scare or frighten anyone; it is a call to arms for governments, people who may have previously had ulterior motives, to unite and to finally wake up to the avoidable but critical disaster and slippery slope we have already created for ourselves, one that is also being greased.

Imagine if our Energy, our food supply chain, our water, our fuel, our banks, and our governments were all simultaneously attacked. No power, dwindling food supplies, no fresh water, and banks shut down due to cyberattacks. Just imagine what carnage, what an uprising such a situation would create. This is no Spielberg movie (although I am happy to discuss), it is a current reality. What is more, it is happening in a town, a city, a state, government, food supplier, trucking company, CI, and water treatment plant near you right now. Our entire infrastructure is falling victim to cyberattacks, and our governments are seemingly helpless to do anything about it. Anarchy is just around the corner, and unless President Biden and his Senators wake up from their slumber and stockpiles of cash and start realising what they are staring down the barrel of, life as we know it will cease within the next decade, and the deprivation, anarchy, and criminal mob culture will take over vast swathes of the world; nobody will be safe, and, from digital innovation to digital domination within three decades, we will see the world's largest ever economic shift and freefall into the hands of cyber criminals.

All-out results call for all-out action, and that is simply not the case, as the war on words continues along with the blame game instead of people, governments, companies, and security professionals doing their jobs properly, and that is to secure their Internet connections instead of facilitating crime. We have shared our vision and thought leadership with CISA and the UK government, and sadly, their heads are so far somewhere they really ought not be, it is clearly masking their ability to see. It is the world's worst-kept secret that the challenges we face today were spawned by the NSA's and GCHQ's methods and tools, particularly post-9/11. Even though I am personally angry about their manipulation, lies, and deception, we are, as they say, where we are. Now we need to urgently address the challenges head on and deal with them not so they can be manipulated further but so we can get the world, our world, and the world of our children back on track and maintain a lawful and harmonious place to live.

Index

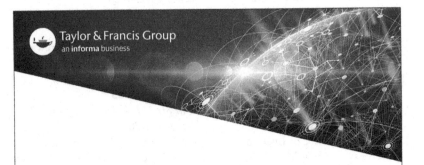

Printed in the United States
by Baker & Taylor Publisher Services